The Sociology
of the State

Bertrand Badie
Pierre Birnbaum

The Sociology
of the State

Translated by
Arthur Goldhammer

The University of Chicago Press
Chicago and London

The University of Chicago Press, Chicago 60637
The University of Chicago Press, Ltd., London

99 98 97 96 95 94 93 92 91   4 5 6 7 8 9

Originally published in Paris under the title *Sociologie de l'Etat,* © Editions Grasset et Fasquelle, 1979.

Library of Congress Cataloging in Publication Data

Badie, Bertrand.
    The sociology of the state.

    Includes bibliographical references and index.
    1. State, The. 2. Political sociology. I. Birnbaum,
Pierre. II. Title.
JC325.B2713 1983   306'.2   92-20249
ISBN 0–226–03549–2 (pbk.)

Contents

Translator's Note

Citations from the works of Tocqueville, Marx, Durkheim, and Weber have either been taken from standard English translations of their works, retranslated from the original French or German by me, or, in the case of a few citations of Marx, rendered into English from a French translation quoted by the authors. The notes will make clear which course has been followed in each instance. For the regrettable instances of circuitous multiple translations of Marx, I apologize to the reader, but it would have cost more time to trace the sources than was warranted by the possible gain in accuracy.

Introduction

In recent years sociology has, in a number of respects, felt the need to come to grips with history. Sociologists, who over the past few decades have seen their discipline achieve the status of a science, have tended to neglect the historical dimension in their work, despite the emphasis placed on history by the "founding fathers" of the field. Two approaches have since predominated. One of these is based on biology and views the social system as an entity capable of maintaining its identity while interacting with its environment. The other has been "microsociological," involving the study of the small groups within which social interaction occurs. Neither approach has encouraged interest in history on the part of sociologists, and neither has given prominence to power and domination. The gulf between sociology and history has been particularly wide in much contemporary American work. Despite its wealth of empirical data, American sociology has deliberately remained ahistorical.

By contrast, French historians, some of them inspired by the work of sociologists, have for the past several decades been using sociological methods to study social history. At present the direction of influence seems to have been reversed. Now it is the sociologists who are trying to integrate the work of the historians into their analyses. Sociology is becoming historical. Sociologists are applying their own models to historical phenomena. This development, which to a large extent began with work done by political sociologists in the English-speaking countries, who were the first to notice the importance of the historical work of the sociologist Max Weber, has stimulated research that has proved surprisingly fruitful. French sociology today stands in urgent need of a genuine rediscovery of history.

A historical approach is needed, in particular, in studying the sociology of the state, which cannot be adequately understood in any other way. The study of the state, which was for a long time left to philosophers and legal scholars, is properly a matter for sociology. This is so not because social factors determine the organization of the state and the way it operates, as certain reductive sociological theories contend, but rather because the state is itself a social fact. An actor in the social system, the state is of course implicated in the history of that system, but at the same time it has a history in its own right.

Only a thoroughly new comparative approach can hope to explain the evolution of the state as an actor in the social system. Such an approach will require the use of various paradigms of sociological analysis to illuminate what historians have managed to learn about the structures of state forms as diverse as ancient city-states, empires, absolute monarchies, and modern industrial states. Historians have, of course, put forward theories of their own to explain changes in the nature of the state, and one aspect of the sociological approach will inevitably be to reinterpret the historians' theories in a new light. This is only natural, inasmuch as sociologists and historians are wont to ask different kinds of questions.

The authors of the present work have had some experience of the methodological difficulties to be expected in taking a sociological approach to history. It is all too common—in France at any rate—to deal with difficulties of this sort by insisting that the sociologist should either defer to the historian or, better still, become a historian himself. Our experience has encouraged us to try a different path. One of us has worked on the problem of explaining political development in sociological terms. The other has attempted to interpret recent changes in the state in France in a fresh light. It is this earlier work that led to the idea of writing the present book. Needless to say, in making the attempt we are greatly indebted to the work of many different historians.

One more thing needs to be said: historical sociology as it now stands is a rather tenuous discipline. It is based on secondhand knowledge of an enormous and rather heterogeneous literature. It makes two large claims: first, that knowledge of the history of various states exists, and second, that a sociological interpretation of that history is possible. Such sweeping claims raise a good many problems, and we do not claim to have solved all of them. Difficulties aside, we have attempted if nothing else to provide a guide to further research and a tentative theoretical model. For in our view there is a pressing need for a sociology of the state that is at once aware of its own origins and capable of investigating the state in all its various forms and (highly unequal) phases of development.

Part One

The State in
Sociological Theory

1   The Classical Theories

Marx's Two Theories of the State

Marx's assertions about the state are of two kinds. On the one hand he states categorically and unequivocally that "the economic structure of society [is] the real foundation on which arises a legal and political superstructure."[1] But when he comes to consider how other writers may one day be able to build on suggestions contained in his own work, he concludes that future Marxists will surely be able to improve on what they find in *Capital* in almost all areas, "except perhaps [in regard to] the relation between the diversity of state forms and the various economic structures of society."[2] How are these two assertions related?

The first is one of several Marxian dicta used by vulgar Marxist theoreticians at the time of the Third International as justification for their reductionist and deterministic version of Marxian theory. In one form or another this version of Marx remains influential today. The same metaphor of base and superstructure, with only minor modifications, is still favored by certain tough-minded theorists who flatter themselves that they have improved on Marx's original formulation by adding references to "the autonomy of the state," "mediations" of one sort or another, or "determination in the last instance." This abstract brand of Marxism has unfortunately become a conceptual game, a machine for producing metaphors. Based on audacious readings of Marx's works, these theories invariably ignore what Marx himself saw so clearly, namely, that the phenomena they seek to explain are extremely diverse in nature. Reductionist theories come in many varieties, but all of them depict the state as a loyal agent of capital. Some, however, are willing to grant capitalists enough intelligence to see the wisdom of affording the state some measure of autonomy, though of course only as a way of consolidating their own domination.

To hold that this was Marx's view is to deny Marx the honor of having been one of the founders of the sociology of the state. In fact, Marx was perfectly well aware that in different societies the state takes different forms. In one place in the "Critique of the Gotha Program," Marx makes a remark that might well serve as an epigraph for the present work: "The 'present-day state' changes with a country's frontier." He adds that the state "is different in the Prusso-German Empire from what it is in Switzerland, it is different in England from what it is in the United States. The 'present-day state' is, therefore, a fiction."[3] Accordingly, one should not speak of "the" state but rather analyze how historical circumstances affect the development of states in various societies. Note that all the states cited by Marx in this striking passage have capitalist economic systems, and yet the nature of the state is profoundly different in each.[4] This crucial point is overlooked by all of Marx's French commentators, whose main concern is to show that his work amounts to a reductionist theory of "economic determinism."

But Marx actually anticipated the sociological approach to the state (to be described in subsequent chapters) to a remarkable degree. For example, he observes that in the United States "bourgeois society did not develop on the foundation of the feudal system, but developed rather from itself. . . . This society appears not as the surviving result of a centuries-old movement, but rather as the starting point of a new movement. . . . The state, in contrast to all earlier national formations, was from the beginning subordinate to bourgeois society, to its production, and never could make the pretence of being an end-in-itself."[5] Thus Marx was aware of the importance of a feudal background, much stressed in recent historical sociology concerned with the origins of European states. In the United States, where the state did not have to free itself from feudal structures, it could not become an "end-in-itself" or claim to be independent of civil society. It therefore remained subordinate to civil society, and, as we shall see later one, the American state remains a minimal one even today.

By way of contrast, in Prussia the state "is nothing but a police-guarded military despotism, embellished with parliamentary forms, alloyed with a feudal admixture."[6] Societies that have known a feudal past thus engender a bureaucratized state capable of dominating civil society rather than a state that is a mere instrument of a ruling bourgeoisie. Because of its past, the Prussian state in the nineteenth century remained "oppressive, independent, a sacred force standing apart from industry, commerce, and agriculture and in no way degrading itself by becoming a vulgar instrument of bourgeois society."[7] None of these passages is ever cited by French commentators on Marx, whose own words stand in such blatant contradiction to their reductive and antisociological interpretations.

Not only in these passages but in many others as well Marx himself offers us the beginnings of a theory of the state that pays attention to the multiplicity of possible historical trajectories. From these various texts there emerges little by little a sociological model of the state that is the diametrical opposite of the all too famous Marxian model of the base and superstructure, with all its reductively deterministic connotations and lack of historical perspective. In Marx's thought it is feudalism, very narrowly defined, that is the key variable in the construction of the state. In other words, before any other sociological writer, Marx himself held that the nature of the state is determined by a socio-political variable and not by the relations of production alone. The absence of a feudal past in the United States accounts for the "subordination" of the American state to civil society and hence to the bourgeoisie. In Prussia, on the other hand, the feudal past explains not only why the state did not become an instrument of the bourgeoisie but also why it was able to press its "claims to independence."

Note that, for Marx, the "independence" of the state is based on its control of the civilian bureaucracy and of a powerful military and police apparatus. In fact, the state can maintain its claim to independence only to the extent that it maintains control over certain specific resources.[8] In Marx's conception, the state is a far cry from a mere condensation of existing class relations. When he actually comes to develop his thinking in terms of political variables, Marx views the state as an institution. "It is," he says, "a great advance to consider the political state as an organism."[9] This "discovery" of Hegel's is essential, Marx believes, because it makes it possible to lay stress on the bureaucracy as the means by which the state attempts to exert control over civil society. Though a materialist, Marx is not disdainful of the supposedly purely idealistic work of Hegel. Here again, an attentive reading of what Marx actually says belies the commonplace interpretation, which is as superficial as it is dogmatic. "Hegel proceeds from the separation of civil society and the political state as two actually different spheres, firmly opposed to one another. And indeed this separation does actually exist in the modern state."[10] Under the influence of particular historical circumstances, the state separates itself out from civil society as a distinct entity, founded on a bureaucratic apparatus. Later sociologists, even more appreciative than Marx of the wide range of actual historical trajectories, reached identical conclusions, backing them up with a more satisfactory typology of the various state forms.

It is of course true that Marx accuses Hegel of failing to see that the bureaucracy can only "defend the imaginary universality of particular interest . . . in order to defend the imaginary particularity of the universal interests."[11] He further charges that Hegel did not reflect on the "content" of bureaucracy.[12] He argues that "the abolition *[Aufhebung]* of the bureaucracy can consist only in the universal interest becoming really—and not, as with Hegel, becoming purely in thought, in abstraction, a particular interest; and this is possible only through the particular interest really becoming universal."[13] As Marx frequently argued in his more programmatic statements, a society reconciled with itself in fact has no need of a state, much less of a bureaucracy. But to focus exclusively on this analysis scarcely does justice to the complexity of Marx's thought. Prefiguring Weber's work on bureaucracy, Marx examines the emergence of "actual" bureaucratic structures in great detail: "State formalism constitutes itself as a real power and becomes itself its own material content."[14] This is the result of "the political revolution." "The political revolution therefore *abolished* the *political character of civil society.* It dissolved civil society into its basic elements, on the one hand *individuals,* and on the other hand the *material and cultural elements* which formed the life experience and the civil situation of these individuals. It set free the political spirit which had . . . been dissolved . . . in . . . feudal society; it reassembled these scattered fragments, liberated the political spirit from its connexion with civil life and made of it the community sphere, the *general* concern of the people."[15]

Weber would later turn to Prussia for his model of bureaucracy. Marx, too, used the Prussian bureaucracy, as analyzed by Hegel, to study the recruitment of bureaucrats, the development of competitive examinations, and the emergence of an internal organizational hierarchy based on competence—all elements that help to make the state autonomous, as modern sociologists have not been remiss in pointing out.[16] Marx gives a very vivid description of the process of differentiation within the state bureaucracy. He then says: "The identity which he [Hegel] has constructed between civil society and the state is the identity of two hostile armies in which each soldier has the 'chance' to become through desertion a member of the other hostile army; and in this Hegel indeed correctly describes the present empirical state of affairs."[17] Hegel, in Marx's view, is no vulgar idealist: his description of the bureaucracy refers to something existing outside his own imagination. In analyzing Hegel's work, Marx even goes so far as to contend that "most of the paragraphs could be found verbatim in the Prussian *Landrecht.*"[18]

Furthermore, it is well known that Marx called Liebknecht a "truly stupid individual" when the latter, in editing an edition of Hegel's works, described Hegel as the man who had discovered and glorified the "royal Prussian" idea of the state.[19] While Marx himself admitted that Hegel's work reflected the reality of the Prussian state, he saw Hegel as the theorist of the bourgeois concept of the state. At bottom Marx's attitude was contradictory, since he acknowledged that in Prussia, because of the residual influence of feudalism, the state dominated society, while at the same time asking, "What remains to the political state in opposition to this essence [viz., private property]? The illusion that it determines when it is rather determined. Indeed, it breaks the will of the family and of society, but merely in order to give existence to the will of private property lacking family and society."[20] An observation like the latter obviously undercuts the sociological model previously elaborated by Marx, in that it blurs the differences between, say, Prussia and the United States. In both cases the state is bound up with private property, regardless of whether or not the state has passed through a feudal stage. Worse still, after arguing, with astonishing sociological insight, that the Prussian state has nothing in common with the Swiss and that both are to be distinguished from the governments of England and the United States, Marx went on to make the following statement: "Nevertheless, the different states of the different civilized countries, in spite of their manifold diversity of form, all have this in common, that they are based on modern bourgeois society, only more or less capitalistically developed. They have, therefore, also certain essential features in common."[21]

Thus, after giving a highly imaginative description of the distinct trajectories followed by England, Prussia, and the United States in their historical development, Marx went back to a mechanistic vision that suffers from all the defects of the views so often ascribed to him, and in so doing he abandoned the subtlety of his earlier arguments.[22] These two aspects of his thought are also visible in his analysis of the Bonapartist state. This work is better known, even if its best passages are rarely cited for the simple reason that they stand in such sharp contrast to the views usually ascribed to Marx. He stresses that in France the "executive power with its enormous bureaucratic and military organization, with its ingenious state machinery . . . with a host of officials numbering half a million, besides an army of another half million, this appalling parasitic body, . . . enmeshes the body of French society like a net and chokes all its pores."[23] The bourgeoisie "apotheosized the sword; the sword rules it."[24] This explains why "the struggle seems to be settled in such a way that all classes, equally impotent and equally mute, fall on their knees before the rifle butt."[25]

Just as, in Marx's view, the bureaucratized state in Prussia had become independent of society, so in France "the state machine has consolidated its position" vis-à-vis bourgeois society and seems "to have made itself completely independent" under the second Bonaparte.[26] Marx repeats this point, which he believes to be crucial, several times: Bonaparte, he says, is "the executive authority which has made itself an independent power."[27] Though frequently disregarded, this part of Marx's analysis shows that he continued to be faithful to his early view that, in certain historical circumstances, the state, by developing a sufficiently differentiated internal structure, can actually separate itself from civil society. Commentators on Marx almost always characterize this model as "Bonapartist," thus limiting its scope. They claim that Marx regarded it as a model useful for describing an exceptional situation, which could be explained as the result either of a temporary equilibrium between the antagonistic social classes (as Engels puts it, "exceptional periods . . . occur when the warring classes are so nearly equal in forces that the state power, as apparent mediator, acquires for the moment a certain independence in relation to both")[28] or of a temporary lapse in the ruling class's hegemony over civil society.[29]

Now both of these explanations rely on infrastructural considerations to account for the independence of the state, an independence that is invariably assumed to be no more than a temporary state of affairs. We think it is more fruitful, however, to consider the whole body of texts in which Marx asserts the historical, indeed the "actual," character of state independence, which he, for one, does not restrict to the exceptional circumstances of the Napoleonic period. In this perspective, the independence of the state may be understood as the result of a general process of differentiation, sometimes occurring in a feudal past (as in Prussia and France), other times not (as in the United States); this process leads to the emergence of a distinct site or locus of political activity, to a division of responsibility as a result of division of labor in a global mechanism. Within the specific locus of political activity, a highly bureaucratic state organization arises.

Marx's exceptionally acute intuition saved him from falling victim to the traditional metaphor of base and superstructure: it is the division of labor, and not private property in the means of production, that accounts for the birth of the state. Later destined to play a crucial role in modern sociological theories of the state, this idea is presented in a particularly explicit form in *The German Ideology*. According to Marx, the division of labor conditions both the formation of social classes and the formation of the state:[30] "The greatest division of material and mental labour is the separation of town and country. The antagonism between town and country begins with the transition from barbarism to civilisation, from tribe to State, from locality to nation." It is of course true that Marx does not approve of the division of labor, because it "offers us the first example of how . . . man's own deed becomes an alien power opposed to him, which enslaves him instead of being controlled by him." Unlike modern sociologists of the state, Marx condemns such a division of labor, which entails structural differentiation and which, as he sees it, prevents society from achieving a reconciliation with itself and moving on to a new form of community. But while Marx deplores the consequences of this sort of division of labor, whose abolition he deems absolutely essential, he does nevertheless take note of its existence. At the same time Marx is even more concerned to mark his distance from a functional view of the differentiated state, despite the attractiveness that such a view held for him. For the bureaucratic machinery that had grown up in France or Prussia in order to assure the state's independence of action had turned out, as Marx saw it, to be profoundly dysfunctional. Far from being the result of a rational division of labor, the bureaucratic state bore the stigma of its parasitic origins.

For Marx, the Second Empire was an "appalling parasitic body, which enmeshes the body of French society like a net and chokes all its pores."[31] Deprived of any social function and reduced to the role of a parasite, the state had fallen completely into the hands of the ruling classes, which used it as a tool.[32] Marx attacked this state repeatedly: in his eyes it was a "parasitic excrescence," "the orgy of all the canonical elements," "society's supernatural freak," "a boa constrictor" whose servants were a "swarm of vermin," "well-paid sycophants" who exploited the people.[33] The bureaucracy, no longer a necessary ingredient of the state's autonomy, now seemed to Marx a mere parasite rather than a guarantor of independence.[34] It may be added that it is hard to understand why the bourgeoisie needed the bureaucracy at all, if it was in fact as worthless as Marx seems to think.

At this stage Marx was no longer interested in the idea that the bureaucracy is an institution that arises from the functional division of labor: he now views it merely as an instrument of the bourgeoisie. This leads to the conclusion that "state power is not suspended in midair."[35] It has lost all semblance of independence: "The state power, apparently soaring high above society, was at the same time itself the greatest scandal of that society and the very hotbed of all its corruptions. . . . [Bonapartism] is, at the same time, the most prostitute and ultimate form of the state power which nascent middle class society had commenced to elaborate as a means of its own emancipation from feudalism."[36] The political sociology of the state has been forgotten, as has the notion that the state's pattern of development is determined by the presence or absence of a feudal past. Marx seems here to agree with Engels that the state "is normally the state of the most powerful, economically ruling class, which [thereby] becomes also the politically ruling class."[37] In the *Communist Manifesto,* Marx and Engels had written that "the executive of the modern state is but a committee for managing the common affairs of the whole bourgeoisie."[38] It would be possible to cite many other passages in which Marx seems to take a reductionist approach to the theory of the state. In such passages the other Marxian theory of the state, the theory that emphasized the state's genuine independence from both civil society as a whole and from the bourgeoisie as a ruling class, seems to have vanished, giving way to the view that the state is but a "servile"[39] instrument of the most powerful social and economic forces. This reductionist view has persisted to this day and has led to any number of economistic readings of Marx in which the state, though perhaps allowed some marginal autonomy, is denied any inherent reality of its own. An evolutionary view of the development of the state is a logical consequence. Since the emergence of the state is associated with the inception of private property and with the resulting breakdown of what is assumed to have been the harmonious existence of communal societies, the state is no longer seen as having any history of its own. Its birth, growth, and decay are all bound up with the fate of capitalism, just as capitalism itself is the successor of ancient slavery and feudalism and must one day give way to communism. The end of the state is identical with the end of capitalist society: "The interference of the state power in social relations becomes superfluous in one sphere after another, and then ceases of itself. The government of persons is replaced by the administration of things and the direction of the processes of production."[40] Thereupon the state must be relegated to "the museum of antiquities, next to the spinning wheel and the bronze ax."[41]

Because the history of the state is bound up with the history of private property (except in the special case of oriental despotism),[42] the state comes into being and develops solely in response to the dictates of capital and the whims of the owners of capital. In this final presentation of the history of the state, then, the state's course of development is linear and always the same, regardless of the particular trajectory of the society within which it first takes wing and ultimately withers away.

Durkheim, the Division of Labor, and the State

Durkheim, the father of modern sociology, is frequently presented as the anti-Marx, the sociologist of conservatism, integration, and consensus. For the naïve observer, Marx is quintessentially the theoretician of conflict, of social antagonism, of ineluctable historical transformations. Durkheim, on the other hand, figures as the apostle of peaceful and stable industrial societies, of societies capable of harmonious development. Marxist theory is thus reduced to the class struggle, and Durkheimian theory to industrial society. Now, as we have already attempted to demonstrate, this description seriously distorts Marx's work. We may now add that it does no justice to Durkheim's either.

It is true that Durkheim, taking a point of view diametrically opposed to that of Marx, concentrated mainly on the analysis of social development due to an increasing division of labor. Marx did not view the division of labor as a crucial variable except in certain youthful works, whereas Durkheim believed that, by itself, the division of labor could account for the transformation of a social system. In this respect, Durkheim's thought was deeply colored by the kind of organicist thinking prevalent in the nineteenth century, according to which social history could be explained by the division of labor because societies, like biological systems, develop as a result of constantly increasing specialization of their organs, each of which is responsible for performing certain specific functions.

Durkheim, however, rightly eschewed strict organicist doctrine, which suffered from drawing too close a parallel between the biological organism and the social body. He showed, for example, how social structures may change their function. He thus put an end to the identification of organs with functions that had served as the basis of most traditionalist, organicist theories, such as those of Bonald and de Maistre. For Durkheim, then, the division of labor became an instrument of modernity rather than of conservatism. Traditionalists rejected the historical transformations that were destroying the old power structure and called for a return to what they regarded as a natural division of responsibilities that made the old order a legitimate one. Durkheim, on the other hand, showed how the constantly increasing division of labor gives rise to new structures and hence new forms of power.

Among these new forms of power is the modern state. Durkheim stressed the fact that "the greater the development of society, the greater the development of the state. The state takes on more and more functions and becomes increasingly involved in all other social functions, thereby centralizing and unifying them. Advances in centralization parallel advances in civilization. One has only to compare what the state is today in a great nation such as France, Germany, or Italy with what it was in the Middle Ages to see that change has always worked in the same direction. . . . No historical law is more firmly established than this one."[43] Durkheim has here formulated an evolutionary conception of social transformation in which the necessary division of labor leads ineluctably to the rise of the state. Aware of the peculiarities of certain historical trajectories, Durkheim, like Marx, does, however, show that certain societies, in which the state developed to a particular degree, shared similar fates. But since he is more interested in the remote origins of social systems and focuses mainly on anthropological works, he is less aware than Marx of the extreme diversity of modern processes of political centralization, and he is much more attached than Marx to a narrowly evolutionary view of state formation. He supposes that all states always develop according to the same laws.

Durkheim sees centralization and state building as identical processes. The necessity of division of labor gives rise to the state. He does not see that, depending on the historical circumstances, some societies may develop a political center different from what he understands by the notion of a state. This prevents him from understanding the differences between France and Italy, for example. Nor does he recognize how both of these countries differ from, say, the United States, a society of a different type.

On rare occasions, however, Durkheim does seem willing to accept a less one-dimensional view. Thus he admits that "not all states are of the same nature,"[44] and that "different types of society should not be confused with different forms of the state: two societies may be of different types and yet governed in the same way."[45] He maintains that history[46] ought to provide the sociology of the state with "useful indications."[47] He asks what it is that distinguishes federal states from other types of states.[48] And he even goes so far as to remark that "the state in Russia is not a product of society but something external to it. The Russian state has always tried to act on Russian society from the outside. The analogy between this situation and the situation in China, as we pointed out last year, is worth noting."[49]

Unfortunately, the nonevolutionary conception of the state implicit in the above remarks is so radically at odds with Durkheim's belief that the division of labor is a uniform process invariably improving the distribution of social functions that he does not even attempt to follow out its consequences. Had he tried to do so, he might have cast doubt on his faith in progress, on his belief that the normal course of development leads to an integrated, harmonious society in which the state plays a specific and constant role.

Durkheim's last word on the state, or "governmental organ" as he calls it, is that it is a "normal phenomenon" that "results from the very progress of the division of labor."[50] His interpretation of social history is well known. In societies where the division of labor is unknown, he argues, solidarity cannot arise from the division of tasks and so must be produced by strong external constraints imposed by custom, religion, and collective representations in general. This "mechanical solidarity," as he calls it, is therefore the result of a large measure of social control. By contrast, as society becomes more dense, division of labor becomes indispensable, and this encourages the growth of "organic solidarity," which is connected with a functional apportionment of tasks. At this point, solidarity becomes a consequence of the interdependence of the social actors rather than of external constraint. The intensity of collective representations decreases, social control loses its force, and the state is free at last to develop as a "distinct organ."

With the state there emerge new legal rules. Thus the growing autonomy of the state leads to the development of administrative law. Anticipating recent work in political sociology, Durkheim observes that "history surely shows, in very systematic fashion, that administrative law is as much more developed as societies approach a more elevated type."[51] Indeed, he says, "if we may again borrow biological terminology, which, though metaphorical, is none the less useful, we may say that [administrative rules] determine the way in which the cerebro-spinal system of the social organism functions. This system, in common parlance, is designated by the name, State."[52]

Taking his cue from Tocqueville, Durkheim traces the history of the state viewed as the unique agency of centralization. He shows how the state "progressively extends a more compact system over the whole surface of the territory, a system more and more complex with ramifications which displace or assimilate preexisting local organs."[53] He further shows how the state gains control over education and communication and how it gathers statistics to help it organize its activities.[54] These functions are part of the state's "normal" activity, inasmuch as the state is the organ of "reflection" and "deliberation."[55] It acts as a "brain," which controls certain other activities.[56] "The essential function of the state," Durkheim tells us, "is to think."

The state is now viewed as the organ of rationality. This explains why it must not trail along after its citizens. The role of the state "is not to express the unconsidered thoughts of the crowd but rather to add to them more mature thoughts, which, precisely because they are more mature, cannot fail to be different."[57] In other words, by viewing the state as a functional instrument, Durkheim seems to be saying that its growing power is legitimate. This explains why some commentators have argued that one can explain the success of Durkheimian sociology under the Third Republic and the reason for its introduction into the Ecoles Normales (or teacher training schools) in terms of its use by then powerful political forces to achieve autonomy and combat the power of the Church: Durkheim's work stood for the uniqueness of the state and for its distinctive nature compared with other forces in civil society.[58] Two important attributes of any genuine state were highlighted by Durkheim's stress on the development of administrative law and the state's struggle with the Church over control of the French educational system. He further indicated how the action of the state helps to weaken the hold of social groups over their individual members. "The essential function of the state," he tells us, "is to liberate individual personalities. Merely by exerting pressure on the elementary societies of which it is made up, the state prevents those societies from using their influence to repress individuals, as they otherwise would do."[59] As he puts it, "the stronger the state, the more the individual is respected."[60]

Thus the rise of the state leads to the emancipation of its citizens, who gain freedom from the control of peripheral social groups and local allegiances as well as from the hold of the Church. Such, indeed, was the purpose of the Third Republic, in which the state fought the Church, sent its schoolteachers to carry the good Republican word to the most outlying provinces, sought to nationalize local politics, and began building a bureaucracy. For Durkheim, bureaucracy "defines the state. The state is a group of functionaries, *sui generis*,"[61] bound together by "authority" and "hierarchy."[62] Like Weber, Durkheim devotes lengthy analyses to the formation of an autonomous bureaucracy, whereby institutionalization becomes possible. He shows how the agents of the state must act according to the "general interest," how even in private life their behavior is determined by their function, and how the civil servant must give priority to his position as an agent of the state over his position as a citizen. Carrying this logic out to the end, Durkheim even opposed the organization of a civil service union on the grounds that a union would have extended claims belonging to the sphere of civil liberty into the bosom of the state, when the state was in fact obliged to maintain its distance from civil society in order to insure that it would remain an instrument of clear, rational thought.[63]

Once the steadily increasing division of labor has made the state a "distinct organ of society," it can then "stand above all other interests," above "castes, classes, corporations, coteries of every sort, and every kind of economic person."[64] Thus Durkheim believed that the progress of the division of labor entails the rise of the state and hence the emancipation of its citizens. By contrast, for Marx the division of labor always leads to alienation. While Marx recognizes that the growth of the state leads to the growth of bureaucracy, he argues that bureaucracy must always be combatted. Furthermore, whereas for Durkheim the normal division of labor enables the state to free itself of all outside control, including the control of any social class, Marx maintains that "all the organs of the state become ears, eyes, arms, and legs enabling the owners of property to act."[65] For Durkheim the state is the functional instrument of modern society; for Marx it is usually the agent of the bourgeoisie. Thus the Marxian and Durkheimian conceptions of the state would appear to be totally divergent.[66]

Yet Durkheim follows both Marx and Tocqueville when he argues that if the state grows too large, it may as a result claim to dominate all aspects of civil society. As he puts it, "a society composed of dispersed and unorganized individuals that an overgrown state attempts to enclose and hold together is a veritable sociological monster."[67] Similarly, in *Suicide,* Durkheim contends that "whereas the state swells to the point of hypertrophy in attempting, without ever succeeding, to exert sufficient pressure on individuals, the latter, not bound together in any way, roll over one another like so many molecules of liquid, [generating] forces that hold themselves together, fix themselves in place, and establish an organization."[68]

Thus Durkheim's analysis turns out to be rather close to that of Marx, who also showed how the state "holds together and protects" all civil society, as well as to that of Tocqueville, who saw "an immense central power, which has drawn in and swallowed up in its own unity all the parcels of authority and influence that were previously dispersed among a plethora of secondary powers, orders, classes, professions, families, and individuals, scattered, as it were, throughout the body social."[69]

In reality, though, Durkheim's view is more an extension of Tocqueville's than of Marx's, because both Durkheim and Tocqueville hold that the roots of despotism lie in the emergence of an atomized mass society in which no primary or intermediary group, no association or corporation, is available to limit the power of the institutionalized state. We see here the full extent of Tocqueville's influence on Durkheim: both are concerned with theories of mass society rather than class society.[70]

By contrast, when Marx, in speaking of Bonapartism, mentions the possibility of a despotic state, he explains how this can happen not by using a mass-society model but rather in terms of a certain set of class relations: for him, the state lays claim to independence by attempting to dominate all the social classes and not by atomizing civil society. Furthermore, the state's claim to independence is only provisional (it being almost inevitable that the state will reestablish a special relationship with the dominant social class), whereas for both Tocqueville and Durkheim the state may act independently for much longer periods. Once society has been atomized, they argue, there is nothing left to threaten the state's independence.

Thus the normal division of labor does not always give rise to a simple functional state. Durkheim recognizes that, despite the division of labor, modern societies may undergo a "pathological" form of development, when class relations remain so unequal that they do not allow a proper correspondence to be established between the functions performed by the social actors and their inherent competence. He argues that, when the division of labor is "constrained" by the perpetuation of fortunes through inheritance,[71] the emergence of a new organic solidarity may be compromised. Now, even though this pathological evolution is not explained, as in Marx, by private property in the means of production but rather by a nonmeritocratic use of talent, the explanation once again relies on infrastructure[72] rather than on the specific historical trajectory of a given society to explain the dysfunctional consequences. Faced with pathological developments of which he himself recognized the possibility, Durkheim was not bold enough to inquire into the political consequences (in either his *Division du travail social* or his *Leçons de sociologie*), nor did he choose to take a fresh look at the nature of the state in such a society. Even though, starting with different premises, he arrived at conclusions rather close to those of Marx (e.g., in showing how, in a society as far from being meritocratic as capitalist society, the state is a far cry from a mere functional organ of "clear thought"), Durkheim did not dare to take the next step. He contented himself with reemphasizing the inevitably pathological character of the state in mass society. He preferred to remain silent as to the functions assumed by the state in a class society. Whereas Marx, by establishing a close link between the state and a dominant social class, gave prominence to one particular model of the state, Durkheim emphasized chiefly his concept of the "normal" division of labor, which enabled him to view the state as a mere functional organ. Now, both Marx and Durkheim had a dual vision of the driving force in social transformation; both showed themselves aware to some extent of the multiplicity of state forms produced by specific historical trajectories. Hence both might have renounced an evolutionary view of history that inevitably leads to a reductionist theory of the state. This same dilemma also confronted Weber and still confronts much recent work in sociology, as we propose to show next.

Weber, the State, and Western Rationality

Despite their richness, both the Marxist and Durkheimian theories of the state remain incomplete for the reasons we have seen. Since the state does not occupy a central place among the concerns of either Marx or Durkheim, their reflections on the emergence and construction of the state as an institution remain tenuous and contradictory. By contrast, the state is a central feature of Max Weber's work, the true fountainhead of modern political sociology.

The great German sociologist was the first to consider political phenomena as specific data with a logic and history of their own. No longer is politics explained, as in the general models of Marx and Durkheim, by the relations of production or the division of labor. Now it contains its own determinants. From Weber's time onward, historical sociology has been called upon to explain political phenomena in terms of a "materialism"[73] based on political or military considerations, a materialism that has turned out to be just as powerful a tool as economic materialism. Change in social systems is influenced not only by the means of production but equally by the "means of administration."[74]

Weber was interested primarily in domination, subordination, authority, might *(puissance),* and power *(pouvoir).* His reconstruction of social history was based on looking at transformation in the mode of government. For example, feudalism can be explained in terms of a certain type of control over the material means of domination, as a regime of private property in the instruments of violence and diffuse appropriation of the means of administration.

French sociology, which has been influenced more by Marx and Durkheim than by Weber, has only recently begun to see much importance in the latter's work. Those French sociologists who have paid attention to Weber have focused mainly on his methodological writings and his view of the social system, on the role played by the concept of values in his thinking, or, again, on his treatment of bureaucracy. Yet a central feature of Weber's work is its systematic use of historical materials. The first sociologist to use history in so important a way, Weber chose to present his sociology of domination and hence of the state in a historical light.

Rather than follow the nineteenth-century theorists in propounding evolutionary models, Weber employed an analytic method and attempted to work out a typological classification. He analyzed social relations that exist to one degree or another in all societies. Initially, at least, he therefore avoided writing history when he studied a society. Instead, he tried to distinguish three main forms of legitimate domination: the charismatic, the traditional, and the rational. Rational domination operates through an agency such as the state. No claim is made that those types of domination succeed one another in any particular order.

This is not the place to undertake a full analysis of Weber's sociology of domination. We need only recall that for Weber charismatic domination is made possible by the appearance of a personage "endowed with supernatural or superhuman strength or character," a person capable of being regarded as a "messenger from God" and therefore as a "leader" *(Führer).*[75] From the first, Weber stresses that the power of the charismatic leader is "alien to the economy." He emphasizes the degree to which this type of power acts without administrative guidance and is therefore to be contrasted with both traditional domination and rational domination. Weber then goes on to consider the "routinization" of charisma, which may, for example, occur when the question of choosing a successor to the leader arises. But Weber rejects any evolutionary interpretation and points out that charismatic power can just as easily turn into traditional domination as it can lead to bureaucratization. There is no unique law of history.

With the aid of a large number of historical examples, Weber also shows how the routinization of charisma allows for an adaptation to economic necessities, though he is far from arguing that such necessities cause charismatic power to emerge. In particular, he spends a good deal of time discussing feudalism as a mode of routinization of charismatic power, drawing a distinction between the feudalism of fiefs (free personal contract) and the feudalism of benefices (which results when social actors arise to meet the economic needs of the lord and which, Weber tells us, has developed mainly in the Islamic Middle East and in India). Historical processes can therefore have more than one outcome.

Weber does not see charismatic domination as something that occurs only in societies remote from our own in time or space. Among the instances of charismatic domination that he cites are the plebiscitary democracies headed by Cromwell, Robespierre, and Napoleon. Thus charisma can play a part even in governments that eventually develop bureaucratic forms of administration. Contradicting one vulgar-Marxist interpretation, Weber asserts that "plebiscitary authorities can readily weaken the (formal) rationality of the economy, even though the dependence of their legitimacy on the faith and submissiveness of the masses forces them, conversely, to use economic means to defend the supposed material bases of justice."[76] Found in all periods of history, charisma is thus a genuine source of power and may lead to changes in the way a society is stratified or, as in the case of antiauthoritarian charisma, to economic measures designed to please the populace, measures that must be implemented by an administration already in place prior to the advent of the charismatic leader. The number of functions that may be fulfilled by charismatic forms of domination is therefore large. Charismatic domination may also give rise to many types of political system. No one type of political system will inevitably succeed a charismatic episode, however.[77]

We have gone into some detail regarding the charismatic form of domination in order to make clear how Weber explains the growth of an institution. Charisma, he argues, gives way to one form or another of impersonal power, and this may in turn be followed by new forms of charisma that can emerge even in highly structured institutions (such as political parties). We hope that this account makes clear the deeply anti-evolutionist tendencies in Weber's thought, tendencies that distinguish Weber's sociology not only from Marx's but also from Durkheim's notion of normal social development.

That said, it remains true that traditional domination, as the name implies, belongs to the past and is incompatible with a modern form of society. It "rests on the sacred character of attitudes transmitted through time and . . . thus accepted."[78] For our purposes, the main point to keep in mind is that traditional domination is frequently associated with the hereditary power of a lord. The lord maintains control over his underlings, whose help he needs to administer his territory, either by feeding them at his own table, remunerating them in kind, or awarding them a fief.

Historically, states arose in connection with efforts to deal with the problems inherent in this sort of administration, in which jobs could be passed on from father to son. The state countered this "patrimonial" system by establishing a bureaucracy based on the "legal" form of domination. This is the third category in Weber's typology, which was intended to avoid an oversimplified evolutionary approach. But the notion of legal domination is in fact colored, perhaps inadvertently, by the sort of evolutionary thinking that influenced most nineteenth-century social philosophy and that continues to be influential even today.

"In every sphere," Weber tells us, "in state, church, army, party, firm, interest group, association, foundation, etc., the development of 'modern' forms of association is quite simply identical with the development and constant growth of bureaucratic forms of administration: bureacracy is, so to speak, the spore of the modern Western state."[79] Furthermore, "the great modern state is absolutely dependent on a bureaucratic basis. The larger the state ... the more unconditionally this is the case."[80] At this point we move into a second dimension of typology. Modern societies are characterized by the emergence of exclusive legal domination, which is revealed chiefly through the formation and development of an institutionalized bureaucracy, literally the instrument of the contemporary state.

"By state," says Weber, "we mean a political enterprise of institutional character in which, and to the extent that, the administrative agency successfully claims, in enforcing its regulations, a monopoly of legitimate physical force."[81] The author of *Economy and Society* includes many passages in which he analyzes at length what he takes to be the two essential instruments of the state, legitimate violence and a bureaucratic administration. He shows how the end of feudalism came about thanks to the concentration of military power and the use of a type of army no longer dependent on ties of vassalage but rather based on the regular payment of wages to the soldiers by the lord. He also emphasizes the way in which the "modern" state "expropriates the independent 'private' forces that rival it in the possession of administrative power."[82] Thus it is possible to argue that, according to Weber, a state comes into being and becomes modern when it puts an end to all patrimonial aspects of office and severs all ties between the performance of civil or military duties for the state and title to the profits derived from the exercise of office.

The birth of the state marks the end of patrimonialism: the state becomes a distinct institution within society. It differentiates itself from civil society and becomes institutionalized. But in order to complete this process successfully, the state must be able to compensate its servants so that they truly identify with their functions and, as far as their role is concerned, sever their ties to other social groups. Weber is aware that only the development of a monetary economy enables the state to pay its functionaries a regular salary: the advent of a money economy is conducive to the destruction of all forms of traditional power. Weber accordingly distinguishes between a truly functional modern bureaucracy and the vast administrative apparatus that used to exist in Egypt or China, for these enormous bureaucracies were still dependent on a subsistence economy. This meant that state functionaries were paid in kind, so that no genuine bureaucracy could develop and the state itself could not grow.[83]

In Weber's view, then, the birth of the state requires an economy of a certain type, but this does not mean that he regards the state in any way as a superstructure. As he himself points out in order to make clear the difference between his view and the various reductionist theories of the state, "just as capitalism, in its present stage of development, requires bureaucracy—although the two have quite different historical roots—so too does capitalism represent the most rational economic basis for bureaucracy, enabling the later to exist in its most rational form by providing, through taxation, the necessary financial resources."[84] The development of the state is not, therefore, simply a consequence of the growth of capitalism or the division of labor. State, bureaucracy, and capitalism can only develop in mutual association.

It should be noted that Weber and Durkheim agree that bureaucracy is a consequence of the increasing division of labor characteristic of Western societies. Both men maintain that the growth of the bureaucracy, and hence of the state, is an effect not of shifting class relations but rather of the West's steady progress toward greater and greater rationalization. However, Weber, unlike Durkheim, examines the division of labor in the political realm as a phenomenon in its own right, rather than reducing it to an aspect of a more general process. He emphasizes the uniqueness of the state by investigating the historical conditions in which it rose to prominence as a peculiarly Western form of political power in the wake of a peculiarly Western process of differentiation.

Thus there is an evolutionary aspect to Weber's theory, which in this regard parallels the theories of Marx and Durkheim. The evolutionary process highlighted by Weber culminates in the state and its primary instrument, the bureaucracy, for which Weber attempted to provide a theory. This is not the place to give a detailed analysis of Weber's theory of bureaucracy. Recall simply that for Weber a bureaucracy is an organization composed of actors. Each position in the organization corresponds to certain functions, and actors are selected to fill these positions on the basis of their personal skills in accordance with criteria of merit and competence. Because men and jobs are impartially matched, authority relations are impersonal and hierarchical. Thus bureaucracy embodies the form of domination earlier characterized as "legal." This legal domination relies on a form of work organization that is at once rational and legitimate. Within such an institution, governed strictly by internal rules, bureaucrats can hope to win advancement by following the rules, and this in turn helps them to internalize their roles.

The defects in Weber's theory have often been pointed out: it does not, for example, account for the emergence of dysfunction or conflict within a bureaucracy.[85] There are two points to bear in mind about the Weberian model. First, bureaucracy as he sees it is essentially the perfect embodiment of rationality, which he believes is the principle that guides action in the Western world. Second, bureaucracy as an ideal type represents a form of domination totally independent of the sphere of private property. Western societies, Weber argues, are tending more and more toward this type of domination and hence toward a new form of legimation. Put briefly, this view entails the belief that bureaucracy embodies universalistic criteria whereby the state can decide how it must act in order to serve the collectivity as a whole, which is presumed to be its mission. Interpretations of Weber's thought commonly rely on this ideal type. His work is therefore seen as a paean to rationality and bureaucratic administration; a rule-governed bureaucracy is said to be the only possible defender of the public good. The apostles of post-industrial society, inspired by Weber, go even further than he does. They assert that rule-governed bureaucracy helps to reduce social conflict. This, they maintain, explains why Western societies are relatively peaceful, and suggests that the Western type of society should be seen as a model toward which all developing social systems must inevitably

paean /piən/ 颂歌

strive. Thus the evolutionism in Weber's thought helps to justify one kind of ethnocentricity.

This interpretation of Weber's thought is a fair account of the ideal type of bureaucracy as it is presented in *Economy and Society,* but it neglects Weber's concrete historical analyses, all of which show in detail, and from various standpoints, how actual state bureaucracies differ sharply from the proposed model. In studying the power structure in Germany, for example, Weber emphasizes the nearly absolute power exercised by the Junkers and the fact that the institutions of the state bear their stamp. He stresses the authoritarian character of capitalism in Germany, which he says is so because "the class of the rural land-owners of Germany... are the political rulers of the leading German state," i.e., Prussia.[86] Thus in Germany the bureaucracy had not achieved independence from property: it could scarcely claim to be the embodi-ment of rationality, as many of Weber's contemporaries still believed.[87] The fact that the society was dominated exclusively by the landed aris-tocracy not only prevented the development of capitalism and the bourgeoisie but also the concomitant development of a true bureauc-racy. His detailed analysis lays bare the close ties between the aristocracy and the state, in this respect going even further, perhaps, than Marx him-self. In this way Weber shows how the "feudalization" of bourgeois capital forestalled the development of an autonomous state bureaucracy and therefore prevented the state from fulfilling its rational function.

In a similar vein, Weber observes that "the high civil servants and mili-tary leaders in Russia were recruited, as in other countries, mainly among landowners."[88] Thus Russia too had an absolutist regime which was not particularly conducive to the development of a truly differentiated state and which, like the German regime, impeded the development of capitalism. This kind of analysis is of course diametrically opposed to the classic Weberian model of bureaucracy. Not only does the bureauc-racy no longer figure as an autonomous functional organism, it is now not even the assured result of the only possible course of evolution.

Weber also moved away from his ideal type of bureaucracy when he pointed out that a bureaucracy could produce pathological effects if it acted outside its own proper sphere. With the aid of a large number of empirical examples, he shows how a bureaucratic administration may come to be politicized and thereby relinquish its claim to act rationally and impartially. In France, for example, the prefects are "political func-tionaries." The situation is similar in Germany, where ever since the time of Bismarck the role of the bureaucrat has been combined with that of the politician. For Weber such practices are aberrant, because by making bureaucrats partisans they make bureaucracy less functional. Weber opposed "government by bureaucrats" on the grounds that "it is in the nature of officials of high moral standing to be poor politicians."[89]

Finally, attention should also be paid to certain other remarks of Weber's, which also belie the all too common tendency to overemphasize the importance of evolutionism in his work. Careful reading of the long essay entitled "Bureaucracy" reveals just how aware Weber was of the many historical examples, some of them taken from the history of Western societies, that contradict his theoretical model. Early on he acknowledges that is incorrect to argue that "every historically known and genuine formation of great states has brought about a bureaucratic administration."[90] As proof he adduces the fact that the Roman Empire was not highly bureaucratized, nor, for that matter, was the British Empire, of more recent date. His emphasis on the English case provides us with a powerful argument against any evolutionary interpretation of his thought. "The English state," he tells us, "did not share in the continental development towards bureaucratization, but remained an administration of notables."[91] Thus it had no large standing army and no administrative law, whereas these features were characteristic of bureaucratized states on the continent.[92] Similarly, he points out that the United States, which had never had an aristocracy, was for a long time able to avoid problems that the German state was forced to face.[93]

What a difference between the Weber who proclaims that "everywhere the modern state is undergoing bureaucratization,"[94] for which he provides a model, and the Weber who paid such close attention to the variety of actual patterns of evolution! Modern political sociology has long been afflicted with similar contradictions.

2 The Failure of Contemporary Sociology

Until recently, most work in political sociology has avoided the subject of the state. Sociologists turned for inspiration to one of the great forerunners, to the founding fathers of the subject, as it were, but in the end they rejected the models proposed by their predecessors. For many years there was virtually no Marxist work in political sociology (with the exception of Gramsci, an isolated case). The Third International encouraged an economistic orientation, and its propagandists generally had nothing to say about the sociology of the state. Nor were French sociologists much interested in developing Durkheim's political sociology: their predilections ran more to the study of primitive societies, religion, education, and even economics. In the Weberian tradition, by contrast, there was always active interest in political sociology, but attention was focused mainly on bureaucracies and political parties.

Consequently, when political sociology began to develop in earnest, largely between the two world wars and in the English-speaking countries, its practitioners had to turn elsewhere for their inspiration. Political analysis was dominated largely by specialists in the "theory of groups," from Arthur Bentley to David Truman. In the model they developed, the state figured merely as one group of actors among others, with no specific prerogatives and no history in its own right. This "pluralism" in political sociology was largely a reflection of pluralism in the society at large, and it was destined to exert great influence in the field despite the pluralists' indifference to the state as an element of theory.

Similar remarks apply to the sociological theories that emerged at around the same time from systems theory and cybernetics. Like the pluralists, the systems analysts greatly underestimated the importance of the notion of power, even when, like David Easton, Karl Deutsch, and others, they tried to introduce the idea of communication into their work. What is more, the systems theorists tend to view the political system as a feature of all societies, regardless of geographical location or historical period. The dubious hypothesis that all political processes are isomorphic made it hard to conceive of the emergence of the state as a phenomenon characteristic of a specific moment in the history of a society. As a result, the state was long neglected as a field of research in Anglo-American sociology, perhaps owing to the influence of a certain image of British and American social development and to the fact that until quite recently the growth of the state in England and the United States was relatively limited in comparison with its growth elsewhere.[1]

During the sixties, however, the state was rediscovered by sociologists working in England and the United States. Much of this recent work is neither eccentric nor superficial. It is worthy of detailed analysis and cannot be dismissed as altogether inconsequential. True, the rediscovery of the state was incomplete. The work was in part a response to contemporary circumstances, particularly the growth of the "welfare state" and challenges to the conceptual shortcomings of a purely individualistic, interaction-oriented sociology. In many respects this new work may be seen more as a corrective to classical functionalism than as a genuine scientific revolution. Although based on certain paradigms from Weber, it failed to profit as fully as it might have done from nineteenth-century philosophical debates. The Marxist contribution, in particular, was woefully neglected. As a result the state was seen as a rational agency, impartial in its outlook and universalistic in its claims. It was all too readily confounded with bureaucracy. But it is precisely the question of *how* the theme of the state was reinstated in sociological discourse that is most interesting to analyze, for two reasons: first, because the effort required deeper historical insight and a new description of the nature of the state, and second, because it ultimately led some sociologists to propound a full-fledged sociology of the state.

The Neofunctionalist Model of the State

Influenced by both functionalism and Weber, the neofunctionalist model of the state was derived from analysis of the process whereby the sphere of private social relations gradually becomes distinct from the sphere of public authority. On this view, the state marks the consecration of a distinct public sphere; it defines its own legitimacy and establishes conditions intended to assure its own functional autonomy. The model also incorporates the features that traditionally define the state. Its initial role is to organize authority relations in the public sphere. From there it moves on to consolidate its position by defining criteria of citizenship. It develops permanent institutions based on impersonal relations, and these gradually come to claim the primary allegiance of the citizens of the state, supplanting local communities and family groups. Looked at historically, the state is one aspect of the rationalizing process that takes place in all societies undergoing modernization. State building therefore plays a part in what functionalists regard as the four central processes of modernization: differentiation, autonomization, universalization, and institutionalization. Accordingly, the state is an evolutionary development, say the functionalists, and the welfare state is the end result toward which political development leads in all societies.

The State and Rationalization

The way the concept of differentiation is used to explain the emergence of the state is typical of the functionalist treatment. For functionalists, of course, modernization, technological development, the rise of commercial agriculture, industry, and cities all tend to foster the development of increasingly specialized and autonomous social roles and organizations. Going a good deal beyond views first propounded by Durkheim, Neil Smelser raises the process of differentiation to the status of a full-fledged "law of transformation" applicable not only to the economy but to all aspects of society, including the family, religion, and social stratification.[2] Authority structures are no exception: as they become differentiated from other structures and increasingly specialized, the state comes into being. Thus the state is seen as one element in the new social division of labor.

At any rate, the foregoing analysis is a rough summary of the views of Talcott Parsons, who, after having paid little attention to the state, changed his mind in the early sixties and accorded it an important place in his theoretical framework. It is worth pointing out that Parsons began to incorporate the state into his thinking in large part after he started working on changes in the economic structure of society. After observing, in 1960, that the old balance between the market economy and the power of the government was shifting in favor of the latter, thereby increasing government participation in the economy and institutionalizing the government's role,[3] Parsons reaffirmed his view six years later, noting that modern society calls for "a reinforced and no longer limited governmental structure."[4] At the same time he saw the growth of bureaucracy as a universal and necessary characteristic of social evolution. So, too, was the growth of the legal system, the market economy, and democratic associations.[5] All these factors finally forced American sociology to recognize the reality of the "welfare state" and, as Alvin Gouldner has aptly remarked, to work out what was nothing less than a sociological version of Keynesian economics.[6]

Now, Parsons did not stop at acknowledging the necessity of a strong autonomous center of political power, which all in all would have been a rather minor contribution to the sociology of the state. Making use of a neo-evolutionary theory of social development, he attempted to interpret the historical process that led to the emergence of the modern state. He thus offers us a description of the origins of the state and an inventory of the resultant state forms, along with a tentative explanation of the process as a whole.[7]

As Parsons sees it, the emergence of the state is bound up with the process by which the political system becomes differentiated from the other social systems and with the resulting autonomization, institutionalization, and universalization of political processes. According to the hierarchy associated with Parsons's "cybernetic model," this process proceeds in a specific, fixed order: differentiation in the social system is immediately conditioned by mechanisms of an infrastructural order, and specifically by the need to mobilize economic resources. On the other hand, the differentiation process is controlled (and in fact made possible) by the cultural system's capacity to achieve the necessary changes and to institutionalize them.[8] On this view of the matter, the emergence of the state as a differentiated, autonomous political structure is thus conditioned by economic constraints, in particular the development of a market economy, which is said to have the effect of destabilizing the preexisting social equilibrium. Ultimately, however, such a process could only occur because cultural resources conducive to such a change existed in Western Europe. This analysis leads Parsons to see Christianity as the "cultural code" that allowed the differentiation in question to occur,[9] thereby encouraging the autonomization and reinforcement of the state. More precisely, it was the Protestant Reformation that was crucial in allowing the political system to become fully autonomous within the social community.[10]

Given these conditions, the functional effectiveness of the state—which Parsons seems to regard as more and more important as time goes by—is bound up with the same factors that allow the state to become differentiated. More than anything else, the result of differentiation is to distinguish the state from the societal community. This first takes the form of the development of a complex and autonomous legal system, which has the effect of establishing a distinction between the individual member of the society and the citizen or member of the political system.[11] It also leads to the formation of a body of public law, which legitimates the actions of the government and establishes the right of the government to intervene in matters of public interest. Finally, differentiation tends to free the political system from the control of particularistic subgroups. Historically, this has taken the form of a divorce between the monarchy and the aristocracy, with the latter tending to fall back on the *Parlements* (in France under the ancien régime, judicial bodies with a quasi-representative function). At this stage of what is a rather subtle argument, Parsons seems to allow for a marked difference between France and Great Britain in regard to the development of the state, in that the differentiation of monarchy and aristocracy was less clearly and less rapidly institutionalized in the latter than in the former.[12] The formation of the state is still connected with the progressive dissociation of the political system from the other systems: this is true of the separation of church and state in the sphere of relations between the state and the cultural system, as well as of the growth of the market economy in the sphere of the state's relations with the economic system.

Parsons thus describes the modern state as the culmination of the development of the political system, which acquires all the elements necessary for effective political action. The required level of political development presupposes full development of the economy and secularization of the society. The state then acquires certain characteristics, which Parsons regards as intrinsic to it. In the first place, it is *functional* and historically does not emerge as a solution except where there is a problem of overall social integration. In particular, the state cannot consolidate its position if its role is one of serving as an instrument in social conflict or of special-interest groups. Furthermore, the state is, for Parsons, a state of *laws*, the result of the formation of a legal system, whose legitimacy rests on a principle of legality. Finally, the state can only be a *democratic* state whose development is based on parliamentary institutions and on the principle of citizenship, both of which are seen as indispensable prerequisites to the full differentiation of the political system from the other social subsystems.

Important as they are, these conclusions do not exhaust the contribution of the paradigm of social differentiation to the sociology of the state. Functionalists combine these results with other important aspects of political development and state building. For example, the effects of the dissolution of traditional allegiances and of the specialization of social roles extend beyond the reorganization of civil society. They also have a direct influence on the development of political relations, by freeing power from its association with old social hierarchies and distributing it among newly autonomous social groups, thereby assuring that power in the society will not be monopolized by any one group. As Shmuel Eisenstadt points out, this change inevitably paves the way for political competition and spreading social conflict. In traditional societies the conditions for these developments do not exist, and in empires the potential for competition is more or less contained within strict limits.[13] At the same time, social differentiation and the expanded distribution of power allow new demands to find expression, thereby politicizing contending social interests. As the political sphere expands to include the entire society, its differentiation is accelerated, with the result that a "populist" mode of legitimation comes to be adopted. All these factors conspire to produce the modern nation-state, which in this view consolidates itself primarily as a mechanism of self-government of the newly created "market" of political resources and as the organizer of political conflict and participation, hence as the culmination of a process of political centralization.[14] Conflict thus plays the role of a stimulus in the development of the state. More than that, this improved functionalist model shows us that the construction of the state is the work not only of elite groups but also of the masses: political centralization is necessary chiefly as a way of organizing popular participation, a way of coping with what is nothing less than a historical discontinuity, which occurs when the political process expands to include demands from all groups within the society. This modification is more a corrective of the original model than a transformation of it: the state is still seen primarily as an autonomous functional element within the new division of labor, whose purpose is to reduce social tension and to institutionalize a new form of consensus.

Moreover, the new outlook is just a continuation of classical functionalism in its purest form, according to which any process of differentiation risks upsetting the social equilibrium, thereby requiring a response to restore the integration of the society involved. The appearance of new activities, new norms, or new sanctions may result in conflict with traditional structures. In any case, differentiation does not necessarily spread at once throughout the society. Thus differentiation itself can be the cause of inequality, conflict, and antagonism between centers of modernism and centers of tradition within the society, making it likely that acute competition will develop between once allied elements now become enemies.[15] In a situation of this sort, the state can be seen as an integrative structure that takes the place of the law and the various social networks.[16] If Smelser is right, the state even shows a tendency to become the primary integrative element, in that it seems more capable than any other element of bringing harmony to the differentiation process and of developing new social roles specialized in enhancing social integration (such as political organizations, labor unions, and above all social welfare institutions and institutionalized means of regulating the economy, to name a few).[17] It is scarcely paradoxical, then, that this sociology of equilibrium and consensus takes a favorable view of the need to establish a strong state to deal with the problems of economic takeoff and accordingly to support the early phases of social differentiation. Beyond that, Smelser sees this type of political system not only as playing the role of mobilizing political forces and neutralizing traditional allegiances but also as an agent capable of bringing new structures into harmony and of reducing the severity of social conflict.[18]

Oddly enough, comparison of this analysis with that of Parsons shows that the differentiation paradigm assigns the state a far more authoritarian and centralizing role than one would think a priori. In both the early stages of economic development and the later, far more advanced phase of the welfare state, this model invests a large amount of political capital in the modern state, on the assumption that the state will use this capital to modernize the social and economic system. As Wilbert Moore has pointed out, the greater the progress toward industrialization and social differentiation, the more necessary the intervention of the state becomes in order to achieve social integration. The state in effect becomes "the residuary legatee of all unresolved social problems."[19]

All these factors conspire to make the state the coercive agent and organizer of a sociopolitical change that the process of social differentiation is unable to bring about in a "natural" way. The importance belatedly granted to the state by the functionalists is thus, if our interpretation is correct, the first really important modification to be made in the functionalist model, which at first viewed integration as a spontaneous, natural property of the social system. Samuel Huntington was therefore not mistaken when he described the strong, centralized state as the price that had to be paid by societies unable to achieve modernity without conflict and resistance from the traditional structures. We are told that the United States and, to a lesser degree, Great Britain were able to avoid this misfortune because they were able to face up to the demands of the differentiation process without major social conflict. In contrast, the nations of continental Europe were unable to achieve the necessary social differentiation, Huntington argues, until they had centralized political power in an authoritarian manner.[20]

This account seems to ascribe a contradictory significance to the state, however. On the one hand, the state is seen as the rational and necessary *outcome* of a universal process of social differentiation. Accordingly, all states should have developed as centralized political systems, and the mere existence of a state would indicate that the society in which it appeared had undergone political development. On the other hand, the state is defined as the instrument that makes full social differentiation possible. Thus where the state is fully developed, we should expect to find particularly coercive forms of domination, whereas societies in which the state fails to develop are presumably suffering from problems, not to say pathological defects, that impede the centralization process.

These two definitions are frequently confused, and this confusion undeniably weakens the functionalist model. The ambiguity involved in the notion of social differentiation is only partially alleviated by the introduction of the further concept of *autonomy*. In the functionalist model, autonomy plays a role complementary to that of differentiation. In talking about autonomy, functionalists intend to suggest that the rise of the state is related not only to the increasing division of labor but also to the fact that the newly differentiated political structures tend to operate according to rules of their own. Because these political structures perform certain functions and maintain control over certain resources, they are, we are told, in a position to elaborate plans of action in a relatively independent manner, compared with the way other sectors of the society operate.[21] Some authors go even further in their use of the concept of autonomy, arguing that the process of differentiation tends to give the political system the capacity to act on its environment in such a way as to exert influence over it and even to control it.[22] No matter which definition of autonomy is ultimately adopted, it must be conceded that functionalist sociologists in general view the state as the culmination of the process of autonomization and hence as a social actor capable of exerting a specific influence on society as a whole for the purpose of orienting and structuring its development.

This emphasis on the relative autonomy of the state should come as no surprise: one has only to recall that Parsons took the view that the state tends to become increasingly specialized in the fulfillment of the goal-attainment function, and therefore that it is the mission of the state to guide social action. The same remark is true of Eisenstadt's model. If the state emerges in response to the need to organize exchange among the various actors holding resources from which they derive a certain amount of power, then the action of the state will essentially be to induce those actors to bring their own private goals into line with the collective goals, to some degree at any rate, and thereby to encourage the distribution of certain public goods. Now the implementation of such a function is, in more than one respect, an assurance of autonomy, for three reasons: first, the central political structures are placed in the position of acting as an arbiter, whose task is to define the "exchange rate" between one social resource and another; second, these same structures are forced to effect, in an authoritarian manner, some sort of compromise among the actors in possession of important social resources in regard to certain goods valued by all (such as the defense of certain cultural values or of the national identity); and finally, the job of defining and articulating collective goals demanding mobilization of the entire society is thereby restored to the political institutions. In situations where sweeping changes are taking place, this last aspect of the state's functional role may indeed allow quite a remarkable degree of autonomy to the political elites. Eisenstadt has no difficulty showing the similarity between autonomy of this sort and the autonomy enjoyed by the charismatic leader, as described by Weber. Subsequently, in accordance with Weber's formula, this autonomy is transmitted via "routinization of charisma" to institutions created specifically for the purpose of putting the newly elaborated policies into practice.[23] This way of looking at the interrelation of different kinds of social resources results in placing a much higher valuation than before on political resources per se. These are of benefit at first to political elites and later to the institutions that carry on their policies. On this view of the matter, the political system assumes a degree of autonomy that enables it to operate in the manner characteristic of a modern state. This brief account of Eisenstadt's views makes it clear why he regards the exercise by the prince of autonomous political power as one of the two features that distinguish empires from traditional political societies and as an essential precondition for the formation of a nation-state.[24]

In this perspective, autonomy of the political structures may be seen to depend on certain conditions being satisfied. First of all, the resources from which power derives must be sufficiently differentiated and widely available. In this regard, the societies which are likely to afford the political system the highest degree of autonomy are those in which religious, social, and economic resources all tend to count equally as sources of power. If one source of power clearly outweighs all others, political autonomy is unlikely. This proviso is intended to account for the differences between development on the Western model, where the various sources of power tend to be of equal weight, and certain other patterns of development, such as that followed by Russia, for example, where the governmental apparatus was dominated exclusively by the nobility.[25]

A (second) prerequisite of political autonomy is scarcely mentioned by Eisenstadt: a high degree of autonomy requires a high degree of competition among widely dispersed political resources. It is useful to compare France and England in this regard. In the French case, the social division of labor was carried out in a society in which there was considerable competition within the elite and in which political resources were widely dispersed, a legacy of the feudal past. It was therefore necessary for the state in France to consolidate its power and intervene directly as an actor in political struggles within the society. In England, on the other hand, the central political powers had virtually no opportunity to consolidate their strength, since they faced an elite that remained relatively unified.

This second prerequisite, which Eisenstadt surely neglects, is clearly important, for it shows that the autonomy of the political system depends more on specific historical circumstances than on the general principles of modernization on which his model is based. This raises a delicate problem, whose solution has an important bearing on the very concept of the state. We may choose to define the state either narrowly or broadly. If broadly, the state is identified with the center of the political system, and the question of its autonomy becomes a secondary one, a mere contingent property. More narrowly, the state might be defined to include only those political systems that meet the conditions necessary to operate in full autonomy.

Taking the broader definition first, the essential prerequisite for the emergence of the state would be the accumulation by the central authorities of political resources sufficient to neutralize the power of peripheral actors in the social system. If Finer is correct, the state comes into being when the center accumulates enough resources to force the peripheral elites to alter their strategy—to cease fighting against the central authorities and to attempt instead to exert control over them. In the case of England, we are told, this shift occurred some time in the twelfth or thirteenth century; the "strategy of control" was clearly inaugurated by the barons with the Magna Carta (1214-16). In France, on the other hand, the process is supposed to have proceeded much more slowly, stretching all the way from the reign of Philip Augustus (1180-1223) to the time of the Wars of Religion (sixteenth century).[26]

If, however, we choose the narrower definition of the state, it becomes clear that the state cannot assume its full autonomy, and hence its full identity, until it has acquired institutional resources whose complexity is directly related to the resistance the state encounters in dealing with the various structures of the society. This leads to the conclusion that the progress of state building can be measured by the degree of development of certain instrumentalities whose purpose is to make the action of the state effective: bureaucracy, courts, and the military, for example.[27]

Clearly, the more complex and highly developed these instrumentalities are, the greater the capacity of the state to act on its environment and to autonomously impose collective goals distinct from the private goals generated within the social system itself. In this situation, the state's autonomy corresponds to a tangible reality. When the competition among social actors in possession of political resources is too fierce, or when their goals are too divergent, the need for integration requires extensive development of state instrumentalities. For that very reason, these instrumentalities are able to act independently, and the pressure of competition within the society tends to protect them against outside intervention. This is just what Bendix tries to argue in his attempt to show that state building and bureaucratization are inextricably intertwined, in other words, that the growth of the state goes hand in hand with the development of a public administration independent of both political competition and private interests, and in particular in full control of the recruitment of its own personnel. This is probably where the ambiguity noted earlier suddenly turns into a paradox. In order to act as a neutral arbiter between the social forces in contention, the state must be distinct from civil society and must be in a position to command the services of a sufficiently complex and well-organized bureaucratic apparatus. But according to the logic of Bendix's argument, this can happen only in societies in which the degree of integration is lowest, and where in consequence the path of development is most tortuous. By contrast, political systems that by all appearances operate more nearly according to a consensus model, like Great Britain's, will not advance beyond a low level of bureaucratization, and the degree of autonomy of the political system will therefore also remain low.

As a direct participant in the process of social rationalization, the state does not simply come into being when structural differentiation has progressed sufficiently far, bringing political autonomy in its wake.

The emergence of the state also implies that the political actors have adopted what in Parsonian terms is known as a "universalistic orientation," which is associated with social change. The crucial distinction between what Parsons calls the "advanced intermediate empires" and modern political systems is that, in the former, the integration "of more particularistic, less generalized structural elements [is] typically incomplete."[28] In speaking of "particularistic elements," Parsons here has in mind both social strata and peripheral cultures. The distinguishing feature of the state is therefore its capacity to establish a collectivity based strictly on conditions of equality and able to discharge certain functions exclusively, thereby assuring that these functions will be carried out in accordance with strictly universalistic criteria.[29]

This characteristic of the state may be seen, first of all, as the indirect but inevitable result of role differentiation. Indeed, role differentiation requires changes in authority relations in the private sphere, in particular elimination of master-servant relations in the economic sphere and depersonalization of social relations in society in general. Once such a sharp break with the past has occurred, people are forced to fight for social equality and civil rights. In the sphere of politics, this helps to form an egalitarian consciousness in the public and leads to demands that the political system be restructured in accordance with a universalistic orientation.[30] At the same time, the increasing differentiation of political infrastructures and the increasing distribution of political resources force the central authorities to recognize the demand for more extensive political participation and lead the members of the ruling elite themselves to work toward this end as a way of garnering the maximum possible political support. This explains quite clearly why the state-building process culminated in the nineteenth century in the institution of universal suffrage. It also explains why universal suffrage was often a policy put into effect by political parties of a conservative stripe.

Much more immediate factors played a crucial role in the process, however. As Habermas observes in analyzing the logic used by what he terms the "bourgeois" state, the state always seeks to structure public space to resemble the private sphere. Hence, just as the private sphere is organized entirely around exchange between individuals and the laws of the market, the political system pretends to function in accordance with certain "objective" laws to which everyone is subject and which accord no privilege to anyone. Thus, says Habermas, the laws of the state are supposed to correspond precisely to the laws of the market: "Neither set of laws makes any exception among citizens or private individuals; they are objective, which is to say that no individual can manipulate them in his own interest . . . nor are they directed at particular individuals."[31] Following this analogy, the legal system is thought of as an extension of public opinion, so that particular importance is accorded to the institution of parliament as the most tangible expression of the truly universal nature of the state. Viewed in this way, the state clearly ceases to be seen as a structure of domination.[32] The state then becomes in large part comparable to the systems-theoretical model, in which political interaction is reduced to a question of equilibrium between the flow of demands to the center from the periphery and the flow of responses to those demands from the center to the periphery.

The assumption that the state embodies a universalistic principle need not lead to such clear-cut conclusions, but it does contain two further implications, which are not obvious. In the first place, it follows that the state, merely by carrying out its function of coordination, tends to give primacy to allegiance to the nation over all other traditional allegiances; as a result, the state works to establish a direct and exclusive political relationship with each of its citizens.[33] Therefore the state cannot allow any form of mediation between its own institutions and the individual subject, whether the village chieftain common in Asian societies or the noble of feudal Europe.[34] Accordingly, groups within the society have no legal identity except that explicitly granted to them by the state. They also hand over all their political resources to the collectivity defined by the state. Robert Nisbet develops this line of argument to explain the disintegration of the Roman family, which he says was due to both the growth of the military and the parallel growth of the Augustinian *imperium* (which was in turn encouraged by constant war). These helped to deprive the family of its traditional prerogatives and to establish direct political relations between the imperial center and the individual.[35] Viewed in this way, the construction of the state comes down to the gradual formation of a new collectivity within society, which comes to dominate all the other collectivities by accentuating its universalistic character and individualizing its social relations.

In a deeper sense, the universalism of the state is reflected in a major change that takes place in the nature of social interaction, which can be seen most clearly in terms of the paradigm developed by Albert Hirschman.[36] For Hirschman, all public behavior can be classified according to the three categories he calls exit, voice, and loyalty. Using this schema, one can follow Finer in arguing that the rise of a state with universalistic characteristics marks a singular curtailment of the possible courses of action open to the public. Exit becomes almost impossible or at any rate is limited to isolated individual acts, such as voluntary exile. Once the political system establishes its claim to be the only rightful public authority, certain types of political behavior can no longer be integrated. During the feudal period, for example, some individuals and groups were allowed to consider themselves exempt from certain types of political obligation: the clergy and the nobility, for instance, enjoyed certain immunities, certain areas were designated as inviolable sanctuaries, and, even more striking, some cities and towns were accorded various privileges and autonomous rights. The right of vassals to defy their suzerain lords and to switch their allegiance from one lord to another or to take part in one coalition after another was incompatible with the very notion of a sovereign state.[37] Accordingly, Finer suggests that the transition from feudal society to territorial state may be viewed as an attempt by new centers of power to impose a new universalistic order by force; in return for accepting the new order, peripheral powers are offered the opportunity to institutionalize their right of protest— what Hirschman calls "voice"—in the form of, say, parliaments, or else to exercise their right of "exit" once and for all by seceding from the new unit (as Portugal and Catalonia did in opposition to the king of Spain).[38] Once the territorial state has been constituted, however, there is no further basis for the exit option. The significance of the center-periphery relationship then changes drastically and becomes much more restrictive, with the center purely and simply dominating the periphery.

Like any other relation of domination, that between center and periphery requires legitimation, which in this instance is afforded by the spread of nationalistic sentiment in justification of the territorial claims put forth by the nascent state. Now, this nationalistic ideology is for the most part concocted out of values and beliefs associated with ancient communal relations based largely on exclusiveness and particularism. In this regard, therefore, nationalism may be seen as the obverse of the state's universalistic character or at any rate as a concession made to community traditions. On this view, the nation-state formula is a compromise, which from an evolutionary point of view cannot be anything other than tenuous. Thus ultimately one of two things must happen. Either states must increase their "range of action," leading to fusion of two or more territorial states, or the basis of territorial legitimacy must give way, leading to a reconsideration of the relations between center and periphery.[39] In either case, the national factor seems to play no structural role in functionalist theory.

The combined effect of the various processes of social change that functionalist sociology views as related to the rise of the state is thus to bring about the institutionalization of social and political action. As an integrative structure within a differentiated society and as an autonomous actor and universalizing influence, the state can consolidate its role only by working toward a substantive reevaluation of the relation between the political institutions and the established social forces. Medieval and modern historians will find nothing very new in this observation, for they already recognize the importance of the role played by jurists and their investigations of Roman and canon law and legal institutions in the construction of European states.[40]

It is hard to pin down the precise meaning of the term "institution" and to identify the properties associated with institutions, even though the concept of an institution is frequently used in both empirical and theoretical work. We may begin with Eisenstadt's definition: an institution is "an entity whose regulative principle organizes most of the activities of its members in a society or a collectivity and in a definite organizational pattern that is closely related either to the basic problems or needs of this society, group or collectivity or to some of its goals."[41] Eisenstadt adds that this organization translates itself in concrete terms into norms and obligations imposed either by force or by the free will of the individuals involved. He concludes that institutionalization is the process by which social models become embodied in stable organizations.

Starting with such a view, functionalist sociology naturally sees the process of institutionalization as fundamental to the construction of the state. This is true, in the first place, because state building is connected with the extension of the division of labor, and a greater division of labor implies a wide range of new activities that institutions are called upon to organize and link together. Furthermore, these changes give rise to tensions and splits within the society, and these in turn make the task of organization even more urgent and in particular make it essential to establish a political center, lay down rules of the game, set up an autonomous administration, and expand the scope of the legal system— in short, it becomes necessary to take a whole series of measures to deal with conflict in some official way as a normal and permissible part of social interaction.[42] Last but not least, institutionalization is seen as fundamental because the emergence of the state, which is inseparable from the wider process of modernization, marks a substantial modification in the "social needs" in relation to which Eisenstadt specifies the orientation of social institutions. The state considerably alters the social equilibrium on which earlier institutions depended. Characteristic of the transformation of social needs is the necessity to face a situation in which change is a permanent feature of social life, so that society must deal with a constantly shifting array of problems and issues. Like the proliferation of conflict, the generalization of social change thus requires institutions that allow a high degree of organizational and procedural flexibility.[43] The notion of flexibility recalls certain of the most important features that sociology generally ascribes to state institutions: impersonality (which allows independence of the prince), permanence (which protects the institution from the effects of political competition), and a democratic orientation (which enables the institution to adapt to the changing goals of the political system). Eisenstadt accordingly argues that the authoritarianism that is endemic in the third world is indicative of governmental underdevelopment and noninstitutionalization.[44]

Finally, it should be noted that if Eisenstadt's analysis is followed out to the end, it leads to the conclusion that the modernization process invariably reduces to the institutionalization of a higher level of differentiation and thus, as he himself observes, to the adaptation of existing institutions and to the organization of the features intrinsic to the political system undergoing modernization.[45] The assumption, then, is that state building, along with all other aspects of political change, is a purely endogenous process, and that the type of state that emerges is purely the result of an adaptive response by the society's traditional institutions.

At this stage of the argument we are led back to Huntington's hypothesis that the more differentiated a society is, the more its survival depends on the proper functioning of its institutions, since no one force within the society is able to exert its power directly over other forces.[46] If we then consider the four properties that Huntington holds to be characteristic of the institutionalization process (adaptability of organizations and political procedures, complexity, autonomy, and coherence) and apply them to the structures of the state, we find that the result of the state-building process is to develop these features to the full.

The first two of these properties correspond to properties we have already identified above: (adaptability) corresponds quite closely to the flexibility stressed by Eisenstadt, and complexity is the political equivalent of the idea of structural differentiation on which the whole model is based. It should be pointed out, though, that as Huntington uses the term, complexity refers more to the American model of "separation of powers" than to the European model of a centralized bureaucratic state.[47] This is confirmed by the meaning ascribed to the term "coherence," namely, that the political institutions achieve an equilibrium based on consensus. Such a construction placed on "coherence" would imply that there is not much compatibility between, on the one hand, the property of complexity and, on the other hand, the property of autonomy, where effective autonomy requires some minimum level of bureaucratization and concentration of the coercive powers within society.

That said, it should not be surprising that Huntington's discussion of autonomy is brief and ambiguous. He is satisfied to observe that the state must not act as the "executive committee of the bourgeoisie" and that the courts must remain independent of the state. As for the factors tending to guarantee the autonomy of the state within society, Huntington merely observes that the more pluralistic a society becomes, the more independent its institutions will tend to be. There is no discussion at this stage of the role of the bureaucracy or of its personnel. It might be argued, however, that the rise of autonomous, adaptable political institutions is greatly assisted by the development of a bureaucracy, especially if the bureaucracy is able to recruit all its own personnel without outside interference.[48] All these considerations would seem to suggest that the full institutionalization of the political system requires state development on a pattern that differs from the American model in many respects.

The foregoing considerations raise the problem of the actual compatibility of the various characteristics that functionalist sociology attributes to the state-building process. In particular, it is not clear that the need for integration is not, in some respects at least, opposed to the need for autonomy and universality, nor can we be sure that the necessity of integration does not in a general way jeopardize bureaucratic rationality as Weber defines it. It may be asked, for example, whether the persistence of patronage relations in many third-world bureaucracies does not illustrate the fact that it is impossible for the state to satisfy the requirements of integration and autonomy at the same time. Similarly, it is possible to hypothesize that the sale of offices on a large scale, as practiced in France under the absolute monarchy, for example, reflects the difficulty of dealing simultaneously with the problems associated with (1) social differentiation due to the rise of a money economy, (2) the need to integrate new elites, and (3) the requirements of bureaucratic rationality.[49]

Taken together, the above observations suggest that it would be wise to exercise caution in using the differentiation paradigm. Among other things, what has been shown is that differentiation by itself cannot fully account for all aspects of political change, much less explain the process of state building. The limitations of the differentiation paradigm are even more important when it is used in an evolutionary context, as many authors have attempted to do.

The Generalization of the State

Clearly, in the model we have just analyzed, the modern nation-state stands first of all for rationalization of social and political interaction. It is thus an indicator of human progress and can therefore be viewed in an evolutionary context. The use of an evolutionary paradigm is not merely a formal device. In a very specific way it complements the description and analysis given above. In the first place the evolutionary point of view involves the assumption that the state-building process is progressive and ultimately leads to the development of a new and more perfect political system. Furthermore, it implies that the modern state gradually emerges as the only viable form of political organization, ostensibly a form that is valid everywhere and exportable to areas other than the one in which it originated historically. Although this second point is often buried in subtleties and sometimes presented in a contradictory manner, it has very important consequences. Simply put, these are related to the fact that this assertion serves as the basic assumption of that distinctive branch of sociological research known as "modernization theory."

Beyond that, functionalist sociologists, by viewing the rise of the state in terms of a slow evolutionary process rather than as an abrupt and more or less accidental discontinuity in the history of certain social systems, have lent credence to arguments put forward earlier by anthropologists. Robert Lowie, for example, maintained that even the most primitive societies harbor an embryonic form of state and that the need for institutionalization of state functions grows as the range of association widens and the solidarity of isolated communities declines.[50] The same hypothesis, which owes a great deal to Aristotelian notions of the city, may also be found in the work of Evans-Pritchard, Fortes, and many others.[51]

This kind of evolutionary thinking has had an undeniable influence on Samuel Eisenstadt's analysis of traditional empires. He argues that the traditional empire lies midway between traditional society and the modern state and that the key characteristics of the empire result from the fact that the kinds of social and political change that lead to the rise of a modern political system have not yet been carried all the way through. In other words, the traditional empire marks an advance over traditional society and is the first step toward structural differentiation and political autonomy. What makes this step possible is the discovery of new sources of power. But the traditional empire differs from the modern state in several respects, and because of these differences its political performance is not fully satisfactory. For one thing, political power in the empire is not fully autonomous, owing to the persistence of traditional modes of legitimation and inertia of the social hierarchy. For another, institutions are not fully impersonal. Finally, the public domain is not governed exclusively by universalistic criteria, owing to the persistence of traditional local allegiances as well as to citizen apathy resulting from the fact that some people either cannot or will not turn to the central authorities to meet their needs. Eisenstadt thus conceives of the traditional empire as a premodern or pre-state form awaiting further development. It is not a specific new development with defining criteria of its own. His argument that it is essentially conflict over newly differentiated sources of power that is the motor of social change may be novel, but in general his work is clearly evolutionist in conception, as his treatment of empire as a study in the prehistory of the state makes clear.[52]

The view that the state somehow transcends the classical political formations is also common in sociological literature influenced by functionalist thinking. Reinhard Bendix's work is a case in point. He links patrimonialism and the absolutist state and goes on from there to depict absolutism as a necessary preliminary to the development of a bureaucracy, which gradually works its way free of social constraints to achieve full autonomy.[53] Similarly, Parsons treats certain societies as "historical milestones" and analyzes them in terms of a classification of performances and qualities that is clearly derived from a consideration of the fully developed modern state. Parsons arrives at a one-dimensional classification of these milestone societies based on the degree of differentiation and universalism they have achieved. In other words, his ordering is based ultimately on the magnitude of the difference between each milestone society and modern society—in political terms, on the difference between the political system in these societies and the modern Western state with its secular politics, system of laws, and democratic participation.[54] Parsons's analysis is nevertheless somewhat different from more classical versions of evolutionist doctrine. Because he argues in favor of cultural determinism, Parsons is quite willing to account for differences between one form of traditional society and another in terms of differences in their systems of value. Thus at comparable stages of development, the Chinese, Islamic, and Russian Empires were all unique and exhibited characteristic forms of their own. This variety indicates, as Parsons puts it, "that there is considerable variability and branching among lines of evolution."[55] Novel as the conclusion may be, it does not change anything of the essential, since Parsons goes on to assert that in the modern era Western society has acquired universal significance and has served to guide the development of all other social systems.[56] Even though social evolution may proceed at first along a number of lines, eventually development must narrow down to a single path. According to Parsons, this happens once the threshold of modernity has been crossed. He thereby reconciles his earlier, more subtle view with evolutionism in its purest form. It follows that non-Western societies must either stagnate or accept the Western model of modernization and furthermore that the only important evolutionary goals are those already achieved by Western societies. Hence the "modern nation-state" is destined to spread throughout the world as the standard developmental model.[57]

The first result of this approach is a set of criteria for distinguishing between politics in the modern state and politics in traditional societies. Gideon Sjoberg, in his study of the political organization of the preindustrial city, singles out the following features as characteristic of premodern political systems: (1) kinship groups bear the responsibility of maintaining order; (2) the criteria of legitimacy in the political sphere are not distinct from other sorts of legitimating criteria; (3) popular participation in the political process is severely limited; (4) particularistic criteria predominate in all forms of collective enterprise; and (5) there is little difference between wielding political power and administering the personal property of the prince or leader.[58]

It is interesting to note that these observations are consistent with the descriptions given to us by the historians of ancient and premodern political systems. If we turn to a work on the political organization of the Greek city-state, for example, and compare the description there with the model of the modern state propounded above, many differences are apparent. In the first place, political life was still subordinated to religion, which, as Fustel de Coulanges argued with remarkable prescience a century ago, was one of the main reasons why Greek city-states were so particularistic and so unable to integrate broad populations.[59] The same may be said in regard to the fact that the political and kinship systems are not clearly differentiated and that political relations are not governed by universalistic criteria, given that in these political systems citizenship was limited to a minority and even the full-fledged citizen was allowed to play only a limited political role. Last but not least, in the Greek city civil society was almost entirely subordinated to the structures of politics, and political considerations determined the organization of civil society down to the last detail. This resulted in a mode of operation quite different from that of the modern state, in which there is a strict duality of public and private spheres.[60]

By comparison with Greek political institutions, Roman institutions were in most of these respects considerably more "advanced," a fact of which evolutionists have not failed to take advantage. They point, for example, to the development of a complex and highly structured legal order, thanks to which the Roman political system was able to act in a "coherent" and "rational" manner. What is more, this Roman legal order was later to provide the basis for the constitution of the modern Western state. The appearance of the *res publica,* moreover, was the first step toward differentiation of civil and political society and marks an extension of the sphere in which universalistic values operated. Concretely, this took the form of an extension of citizenship and an easing of restrictions on the acquisition of citizenship. The extent of these evolutionary developments was nonetheless limited by the persistence of premodern characteristics in Roman politics. The citizenship role was institutionalized only to a limited degree and remained highly formal; the exercise of rights of citizenship was hampered by the system of property qualifications and emptied of its content by the rapid formation of a ruling class with almost hereditary title to power and a highly particularistic outlook.[61] The differentiation of political structures remained limited, and this considerably impeded the development of a bureaucracy. Particularly noteworthy in this regard is the fact that military, administrative, and judicial offices were often held by a single individual, a situation that gave rise to a high degree of horizontal integration of these distinct organizations, thereby limiting their autonomy and impeding institutionalization. Finally, although universalistic values were promoted in the Roman political system, there was still considerable opposition to them in reality: the power of the family head remained considerable, and many segmental peripheral communities retained their autonomy, thereby impeding the process that is "normally" supposed to eliminate all forms of mediation between the state and the individual.

If one holds to this line of argument, it is not hard to see that the same conclusions can be drawn in regard to non-Western empires, which in an evolutionist perspective are even farther removed than Rome from a modern form of political organization. Thus the Chinese empire, despite the existence of a unified and coherent bureaucracy, exhibited little differentiation in its political and cultural systems. Among other things, this meant that there was only limited autonomy in the recruitment of officials and that a classical education counted for more than professional competence. To this must be added the fact that the hereditary aristocracy remained powerful to a certain extent in that high officials were forced to negotiate with members of the aristocracy concerning the collection of taxes. Then, too, there was no universalistic legal order and little autonomy in the economic sphere. This leads Eisenstadt to the conclusion that ancient China had only begun to develop new sources of power outside the spheres of politics and culture. There was only limited communication between the center and the periphery, and the system's adaptive capabilities were modest.[62]

Turning now to an empire that was based on a different cultural code, the Islamic empire of the Abassids was, despite its centralization, just as different from the modern state as were the Roman and Chinese empires. One reason for this was the patrimonial character of the central bureaucracy, but even more important was the limited differentiation of political and religious structures, which led to identification of the political community with the community of believers *(Umma),* thereby robbing the distinction between the temporal and spiritual powers of any foundation[63] and making even the idea of a state distinct from civil society inapplicable. The fusion of temporal and spiritual powers was all the more complete because of the nature of Islam: a religion without sacramental functions and without even the right to elaborate its doctrine, Islam does not assign itself the mission of mediating between God and man and has consequently never been able to establish itself within society as an organized, hierarchical, and specialized structure; on the other hand it constantly thwarts any desire to establish an autonomous temporal sovereignty over civil society, not to mention a sovereign state. Under these conditions political integration in the Muslim world has always been accomplished by means of "dedifferentiation" of the most thorough sort—in other words, on the basis of each individual's consciousness of participating in the same faith, a consciousness rounded out, in hellenizing Islamic tradition,[64] by reference to the idea of the natural harmony and complementarity of human needs. Not only are all these tenets inconsistent with the principle of citizenship, but they work against the idea that the Islamic empire is limited to any specific territorial base and for that reason have made it difficult for empires based on Islamic culture to claim a legitimate monopoly of political power. Similarly, these kinds of beliefs have prevented the elaboration of an autonomous, institutionalized legal system. Based on precepts from the Koran rather than on general, clearly defined positive principles, the normative systems of Muslim societies have traditionally been inextricably intertwined with the religious system. Thus the norms have been open to multiple interpretations by different sects, limiting both their "coordinating capacity" and their universalistic character. In the East during the Middle Ages, moreover, universalism was further limited by the extraordinarily strong resistance of local particularisms and communal allegiances, which contributed to the proliferation of autonomous sects and to the rise of regional powers independent of the central authorities.

Other consequences may have been even more important: for instance, the interweaving of the public and the private was consecrated by the system of property that held sway in the Abassid era. The Caliph was in fact the sole owner of all land on behalf of the *Umma*. This meant that the private sphere was limited to the narrow area of commercial activities in the cities. Not only was this practice directly opposed to the principle of differentiation, it also made it possible for the Caliph to distribute land *(eqta')* to his lieutenants, who thereby obtained not only the benefit of what the land produced but also territorial sovereignty.[65] This in turn threatened to limit the Caliph's own power, besides which civil society lost its main resource for maintaining its independence from the political system.

The important role that the system of property and socioeconomic power generally seem to play in the development of the state accounts for the weakness of the evolutionists' position, for they tend to see the modern state as the unique outcome of the process of rationalization without viewing that process in relation to a specific mode of appropriation. Even more serious, perhaps, is the likelihood that it is impossible to account for the differences between the Abassid and Chinese empires and modern Western societies in terms of a one-dimensional hierarchy: the Chinese and Islamic empires were not only "less differentiated" than modern Western states, they were also organized in relation to a concept of the sacred that influenced social life at every level and that could only give rise to innovation and adaptation to modernity in a manner that cannot in all respects be reduced to Western patterns of sociopolitical change.[66] Though the concept of differentiation may have a genuine heuristic value, at this stage of analysis it does not seem possible to claim that it has explanatory or predictive capability.

The ethnocentrism of functionalist sociology has had a direct influence on contemporary politics, moreover, in that the tendency has been to view the Western nation-state as the only possible model for the "political modernization" of third-world societies and the only possible goal of the developmental process.[67] Fundamental to classical development theory, this assumption has been revived by the work of Shils and Almond, for whom the notion of a "developed" political system is defined by the modern Western state.[68] Still more bluntly, Lucien Pye argues that the nation-state as it developed in Europe is now spreading throughout the world as the only possible solution to the problems of development. The various crises experienced by young nations are according to Pye mere necessary stages along the way to acquiring the characteristic features of the modern state.[69] Moreover, most recent work in development theory has been based in large part on the differentiation paradigm, elaborated essentially by authors affiliated with the functionalist school. Indeed, the description of the "center" in much of this work is suspiciously reminiscent of the modern Western state.[70]

Even the most clear-sighted functionalist writers have given a picture of the modern nation-state that is at best incomplete, occasionally ambiguous, and usually rather idyllic. Specifically, the state is described as a rational, universally valid solution to the problems of society. It is said to provide a consistent unifying concept for understanding contemporary politics. In this regard it is significant that Edward Shils, who believes that the Western state model has already become a universal reality, draws the conclusion that the major problem for the developing societies of the third world is to organize themselves in ways compatible with the political structures they have already acquired and thereby to achieve integration based on the individual as the fundamental social unit and on consensus as to social goals.[71] It is surely here that the ideological content of the functionalist model is most readily apparent. But it would be a dangerous mistake to take the view that there is nothing but ideology in the model. Sociology will suffer greatly if no attempt is made to extract from functionalist theory what may be useful in working toward a more historical approach to the sociology of the state.

Toward a Critique of the Functionalist Model

It would be pointless to reject the functionalist developmental model in toto. And it would be equally silly to take the easy way out and criticize functionalism by contrasting its model with another model derived from sociological theory of some other stripe. Instead, we propose to take a careful look at the functionalist model in order to see what parts of it might be useful for constructing a sociological explanation of both the origins of the state and its functions. This explanation should be based on a critique of the functionalist model from within, a critique that is as strenuous as we can possibly make it. What we are proposing is more than a merely formal critique. As we have already seen, the functionalist model suffers from a number of contradictions and ambiguities. In particular, the notion of the state as such is confused with the broader notion of a centralized political system. Even more important are the defects and weaknesses of the central concept of differentiation and of the assumption that any apparently "rational" and effective social construct can be extended as such to all contemporary societies.

Critique of the Sociology of Differentiation

The notion of differentiation, which figures in more than one sociological tradition, has an undeniable theoretical and heuristic importance. Nevertheless, its use as a tool for understanding the formation of the nation-state raises problems at a number of levels and frequently fails to address the real questions, sometimes falsifying the historical picture by trying to make the concept carry more weight than it can bear.

Whereas the concept of differentiation was introduced into sociology essentially as a way of describing one aspect of sociopolitical change, the neofunctionalist school has raised its status to that of a fundamental principle underlying its theory of change, thereby harking back to the organicist and evolutionist traditions in their most classical forms.[72] Accordingly, the state is classified as one of the products of an immanent and endogenous social growth, which is seen as uniform, continuous, and teleologically directed. The state is seen not as a historical artifact but rather as a stage—indeed, as the ultimate stage—in an evolutionary process whose tendencies are described in terms of postulates that have already been shown by sociological criticism to be false or at any rate unprovable.[73]

This approach is vitiated not only by theoretical flaws but also by the fact that in many respects it leads to contradictions with what the historians have to tell us. Seeing the state merely as the result of full development of political structures inherent in "traditional societies" commits an author like Eisenstadt to a drastic form of reductionism, wherein the astonishingly complex political life of each traditional empire becomes a mere episode of universal history, whose mantle in some vague way devolves first on one empire, then on another.[74] Such a view obscures or underestimates the fact that the state is born of a combination of factors, some intrinsic, some extrinsic to the society associated with it: most historical work on the state, for example, emphasizes the importance of the feudal past and of socioeconomic change,[75] while taking note of the contribution of the international economic system,[76] the diffusion of Roman law,[77] external military pressure, and internal migration.[78] The process of political differentiation that underlies the formation of the state is therefore exogenous just as much as it is endogenous, and it is characterized by discontinuity just as much as by continuity. What is more, the emergence of the state should be seen as a specific resolution of a specific crisis, a crisis that is in each case peculiarly characteristic of the development of a particular society and not the mere working out of the political aspect of a universal process of social "maturation."

Furthermore, the way the functionalists use the notion of differentiation comes dangerously close to an interdependence model that is more than a little mechanical in conception. Contrary to assertions made by Parsons and Smelser, there is no reason to believe that acceleration of the division of labor in one sector of society must automatically have an impact on all the other sectors, nor that a system that experiences difficulties of adaptation will automatically respond by moving toward greater complexity. Certain institutional spheres—not necessarily the same in all societies—may in fact resist the "requirement" that the system adapt, thereby producing "modern" political systems that vary in type of differentiation from one society to the next: witness the wide variety of relations between the bureaucracy and the political authorities that we find in different modern states, or, again, the variety of relations between the executive and legislative branches or between the state and religious institutions or between the economy and the polity.[79] Great Britain, which is generally regarded as one of the most modern and highly differentiated of states, nonetheless has a political system that in many respects is imperfectly differentiated from the "establishment" and the Church of England. Germany, too, is characterized by the existence of highly differentiated political structures, and yet there is much permeability in both directions between the high ranks of the civil service and the political sphere.[80] This remark is reinforced by the more general observation, made by a number of sociologists, that role differentiation in the economic sphere need not entail a corresponding differentiation of social roles, and that industrialization may well come about, as in India, without causing the traditional family to disintegrate.[81] While it may or may not be true, as Ernest Gellner thinks, that the process of differentiation has given rise to a Western "code of development,"[82] it seems to be much more difficult for differentiation to take place in other societies, though we may not on that account attribute the difficulty to some form of "underdevelopment."

Beyond the fact that the notion of differentiation has been used in a general theory of doubtful validity, functionalist sociology has tended to associate differentiation with rationalization in a manner for which there is no a priori justification. As Clifford Geertz has noted, social and economic role differentiation in present-day Indonesia can hardly be said to have had rational and universalistic consequences: role differentiation may well, on the contrary, reinforce the rigidity of certain aspects of the social system and worsen living conditions for much of the populace.[83] More generally, unlimited division of labor most often leads to professionalization and to increasing fragmentation of knowledge: the danger then is one of consolidation of the elites, decreasing citizen participation in government, and a situation in which the bureaucratic apparatus defines and works toward goals of its own rather than collective goals. When growth and differentiation of state organisms follow in the wake of this kind of development, the result is to impede the achievement of social relations based on universalistic criteria and a rational goal-orientation, which is what growth and differentiation are supposed to promote.[84]

The same criticisms hold good when it comes to the hypothesis that differentiation invariably comes about as a way of resolving tensions in the social system. As Alvin Gouldner has pointed out, any process of differentiation inevitably casts doubt on the validity not only of the system of role distribution but also on the power structure and in some cases on large parts of a society's system of values.[85] This is another way of saying that differentiation threatens to exacerbate existing conflicts and to stir up new conflicts as well as to create new problems of adaptation that institutionalization alone may not succeed in resolving.

There is no doubt, for instance, that the emergence of the state and of centralized bureaucratic structures in Renaissance France cannot be seen simply as a remedy for tensions that existed within feudal society but must be studied more generally as something that could occur only at the expense of the older power structures, which were ultimately done away with. The proof of this contention lies in the fact that the state-building process, which lasted from the fourteenth to the eighteenth century, gave rise to numerous conflicts that ended only with the Revolution of 1789, that is to say, with the total victory of the new order over the old in a violent upheaval.

Worst of all, functionalists considerably overestimated the explanatory capability of the concept of differentiation, and they were unable to avoid certain of the ambiguities associated with its use.[86] When the emergence of the state is said to be a result of structural differentiation within a society, does this mean that the state can emerge only when a certain level of division of labor has been achieved? Or that the state can consolidate its power only through the process of division of labor, at whatever stage that process has reached? Or that the state emerges when a threshold level of differentiation is achieved within the *political* structures of the society, regardless of what is happening in other areas? Since, moreover, differentiation is found in traditional as well as modern societies, is it being suggested that "modernization" was underway in all periods of history and thus that all societies have experienced the "impulse" to construct a state to rule over them, or, alternatively, that the state can come into being only as a result of a modern form of the differentiation process? Here again it seems that there is some confusion between, on the one hand, the idea that the division of labor associated with industrialization required the emergence of authoritarian coordinating structures and hence of a political center, and on the other hand the idea that the emergence of a political center in turn produced further differentiation and extended the process of differentiation to the political sphere. In the strict sense only the latter case can be subsumed under the rubric "state building," and one of the primary goals of the analysis must be to explain why this turns out to be the end result of the role-specialization process in certain societies.

The foregoing discussion shows that differentiation should not be viewed as an independent variable and that the concept has an operational value only when it is seen in the context of actual social processes, which must be brought to light in the course of the analysis. So far as we are concerned, it is the mechanism that controls differentiation, and

not differentiation itself, that explains the birth of the state. Wh
looked at in the broadest possible terms, it becomes apparent that d..
ferentiation is not the only instrument of change and that change often
comes about as a result of the combined effects of dissociation and
association. In this connection Fred Riggs has observed that modern
society was built on role differentiation in industry combined with
"dedifferentiation" and therefore simplification in agriculture.[87] Relying
on the work of a number of historians, Tilly has made a similar observation: namely, that the rise of industrial society came at the cost of
"pastoralization" and "devolution" in the countryside (where devolution is defined as a regressive process affecting all or part of a society,
especially in regard to adaptive capacity, universalization, and differentiation).[88] Clifford Geertz has gone even further, demonstrating that in
Indonesia the growth of a modern, differentiated industrial sector
required reinforcement of the traditional, community-based rural sector, whose function can hardly be seen as transitional.[89] What all of
this suggests is that a thorough sociological account must include not
only differentiation but also the whole range of devolutionary as well as
evolutionary mechanisms. Such an account must therefore reveal the
factors responsible for structuring these mechanisms and for determining their functions and limits.

The cases that have been studied in this light seem to indicate that
the factors in question have to do with the nature of tradition, with the
conflicts brought about by social change, and above all with the power
structure of the society in question. This last dimension is entirely
lacking in the functionalist model, though it emerges quite clearly in
Geertz's discussion of devolution in the case of Indonesia. Ultimately,
the explanation of how a modern industrial sector controlled by for-
eigners can coexist with a traditional, dedifferentiated rural sector that
enables the modern sector to function relies on the nature of the Indo-
nesian power structure.[90] If the sociology of the state is to be based on
the concept of differentiation, it must therefore determine what types
of dedifferentiation and devolution are sanctioned by the newly born
state. It must also look to tradition and study social conflict and the
power structure in order to find an overall explanation for these various
processes.

In constructing a theory of state building, then, we cannot agree
with Eisenstadt that the only phenomena that run counter to differentiation are breakdown, failure, and stagnation and that it is therefore
these phenomena that must be responsible for the "temporary" estab-

lishment of authoritarian, dictatorial, and regressive power structures.[91] Apart from the fact that such phenomena need not work against differentiation, it is also true that the rise of the state is itself inextricably bound up with the effects of certain devolutionary mechanisms. Confining his attention to the history of the West, Tilly in fact shows that the rise of the state went hand in hand with a decline in the importance of traditional representative bodies, such as communal and regional assemblies. Furthermore, the consolidation of the state resulted in the *disappearance* of a great many social roles, from tribal chieftain to castellan.[92] This observation supports the idea that the state should not be viewed theoretically as the outcome of a linear process of differentiation. It further suggests several factors that may be of use in explaining the degree of state building actually achieved: the degree to which the state infringes upon other areas of society varies with the degree of difficulty experienced in converting traditional sociopolitical structures into modern structures and with the degree to which the conversion process is blocked by existing power relations and accompanied by devolutionary phenomena. It is significant in this regard that devolutionary reactions were far less common in England than in France. In England, traditional political structures were able to keep on functioning as intermediaries between the central authorities then coming into existence and the rest of society, and the British state is accordingly less developed than states on the Continent.[93] Thus the explanation of the emergence of the state (in the narrow sense) should be based on a detailed analysis of the previous power structure, (taking account of its rigidity and internal crises) as much as on consideration of the novel conditions associated with an increasing division of labor and industrialization. An explanation in these terms suggests that the state comes into being not so much to sanction social differentiation as to deal with devolutionary processes in areas where the society experiences difficulties in adapting to change.

It is not enough, however, to couple differentiation with dedifferentiation to account for the rise of the state. Amitai Etzioni has shown that the process of state building is also related to another process of social change, which he terms "epigenesis."[94] Social structures do not change only by splitting in two so that each half may assume responsibility for a more highly specialized social function. They may also evolve by joining with other structures or by incorporating new structures so as to carry out functions that did not exist, even in embryonic form, in the previous historical situation. In many respects the rise of the state

epigenesis

can best be described in terms of this kind of model: even if the emergence of the state marks the achievement of a higher degree of differentiation in the political system, it also presupposes the unification of previously dispersed regional and local power centers along with the concomitant formation of political and administrative institutions associated with entirely new functions (such as diplomacy and tax collection). A similar conclusion emerges from a number of works in historical sociology. Certain of these works observe that the formation of the nation state may be viewed as the natural outcome of a segmental feudal system in which lord was pitted against lord in such a way that ultimately one of them was destined to eliminate his rivals and gain a monopoly of political power. Others take a somewhat different tack, pointing out that the Renaissance state was above all the result of a coalition of feudal lords and hence of an alliance of special interests.[95]

When this new dimension is incorporated into the theory, two implications follow. If the state results from the fusion or coalition of social forces and is not merely the outcome of a purely rationalizing process operating in the political sphere, then it follows that it is wrong to regard the state a priori as a neutral and completely autonomous arbiter. Rather, it must be seen in relation to social conflict and as more or less dependent on certain special interests. Etzioni further suggests that epigenesis can take place only in conjunction with the use of power, to control the accumulation and orientation of new structures and functions.[96] Having said this, we may further postulate that the power of the state is also bound up with the power wielded by the men whose special function is to run it, and that the exercise of state power therefore reproduces a political class that stands as one more intermediary between the state's universalistic ideal and the actual conditions under which it must operate.

By analyzing the various mechanisms of social change that are associated with the rise of the state, we can move toward the kind of sociological account we are after. What has been established thus far indicates that the mechanisms in question produce two results: first, by operating through the state they create a "mobilization structure" whose purpose is to compensate for the effects of the social division of labor, and second, they help the social coalition that supports the state to achieve some of its own goals. This interpretation leads to a number of conclusions. First, the birth of the state creates new powers that did not previously exist and does not result merely in the transfer of powers

iously wielded by dispersed political entities. These additional new
~~~ers play a role whose importance depends on the historical circum-
ᵤ.ᵤ.ᵤces attending the centralization of political structures as well as on
the importance of the new social functions for which the state must
assume responsibility. The degree of importance of these new powers
may therefore be taken as a variable that can be used to distinguish
between contemporary political systems, and, in particular, to distinguish between a state in the strict sense and the vaguer notion of a
political center. At the theoretical level, this variable has affinities with
certain aspects of Parsons's concept of power. For example, Parson
rightly rejects the view that power is a zero-sum game. Hence the argument made by some functionalists that the state is merely the result of
a reorganization and redistribution of political power in response to the
social division of labor is clearly false.

As an autonomous source of power, then, the state is also a stake in
political conflict rather than a means of reconciling conflicting interests.
Neofunctionalist sociologists err in arguing that the nation-state is a
perfect functional substitute for vanished community solidarities and
traditional forms of spontaneous accord, and, further, that the state
serves to organize a new consensus in response to the division of labor.[97]
This is an organicist position, and it is unacceptable on two counts: first,
because state building through epigenesis and thus through the fusion
of special-interest groups makes it impossible for the political power
structure to reproduce a previously existing social consensus, and second,
because once the state becomes an autonomous power center, with
access to previously unavailable sources of power, it becomes a target
of political action, an objective to be seized by every organized group
that wishes to impose its own ends on society as a whole. The state thus
tends not to quell conflict but to exacerbate it. The state itself becomes
an additional bone of contention. By hastening the demise of traditional
social structures, the mere formation of an autonomous political center
brings previously dominated social forces into the political struggle,
encouraging them to organize and to put forward political demands of
their own. One striking example of this phenomenon occurred in the
nineteenth century with the formation of workers' political parties in
Europe. At this point the state became not only "functional," in the
sense of spanning the divisions within the society and organizing the
"political marketplace," but also "dysfunctional," in that it gave rise
to new conflicts and became an issue of political struggle.

This last remark casts doubt on the hypothesis that the emergence of the state marks the completion of the differentiation of polity from society or of the "public" from the "private" sphere. As Jürgen Habermas has pointed out, the attempt to establish a sharp distinction of this sort runs into a number of obstacles that emerge clearly as soon as one abandons the dubious notion that civil society is based on a natural or spontaneous consensus of some sort in favor of the more realistic hypothesis that all social interaction evinces conflict of interest. Assuming that this is so, the principle of differentiation enunciated by the functionalists runs into difficulties no matter which "scenario" of development we choose. There are only three possibilities. Either civil society is capable of settling whatever conflicts of interest arise within it on its own, in which case there is no need for the state, since its functions can be taken over by some private power. Or the public authorities will intervene on their own initiative to settle conflicts of interest in such a way as to favor some particular interest, thereby restoring economic order: the state has then been effectively taken over by a private interest. Or else the state may turn first to one private interest and then to another in attempting to act on civil society. It will do this not only to garner maximum support for the political class but also to insure the survival of the system. In this case the state must among other things work out the respective rights of each of the various interest groups within society; in other words, it becomes necessary to subject an important area of civil society to the control of the government.[98] Whichever of the three descriptions seems most correct, it is necessary to modify the idea of differentiation in fundamental ways.[99] And while we are on the subject, it is worth considering the historical significance of the three "scenarios" described above: to what do they correspond, if not to three successive phases in the history of the West, first liberalism, then interventionism, and finally the welfare state?

It should therefore come as no surprise that functionalist sociology, after ignoring what was ambiguous about the liberal state and neglecting the all too glaring deficiencies of the interventionist state, is now hastening to make up the ground it has lost by focusing its attention on the welfare state. Functionalists claim that the welfare state demonstrates the neutrality of the political system as well as its conciliatory and redistributive role. Even if such a thing as a "class state" did exist in the past, the functionalists tell us, the welfare state is supposed to prove that the advent of the postindustrial age has brought with it the triumph of what some in the West would call the "people's state," which elects "policies" designed to minimize or eliminate social problems stemming from the existence of inequalities of power.

This recent turn in funcionalist thinking has helped to reorient sociological debate to focus on the issues of "nondecision" and "avoidance."[100] Some have argued that even though the state is forced to choose policies intended to reduce certain kinds of inequality in order to insure the "survival of the existing system," it is still able to maintain its class character, or at any rate its commitments to certain special interests, by acting in a selective manner and avoiding action in certain key areas or even making action in such areas illegal. Within this framework Claus Offe has no trouble showing that neofunctionalist sociology, with its behavioral outlook, cannot possibly hope to show that such power-related phenomena exist.[101] Now, it is true that the possibility that state institutions may be selective in their policies owing to the influence of certain special interests must be taken into account, and that one must allow for the further possibility that those areas in which the right of the state to intervene is acknowledged are, as Offe maintains, precisely those that do not cast doubt on the established order and particularly on the notion of private property.[102] At the same time, it should be borne in mind that the need to maintain social control makes it virtually impossible to challenge certain social values, and that there are political processes that are able more or less indefinitely to prevent most decisions of a nature to undercut the fundamental principles on which present-day societies are based.

That said, the wish remains that some effort might be made to verify hypotheses of this sort empirically, and that those who believe them to be true not stick to the alibi that phenomena of the kind described are by definition hidden. There is further cause for regret in the fact that Offe's argument casts doubt on the idea that the state is autonomous only to replace it with the idea that it is only "relatively" or "functionally" autonomous, which has the disadvantage of being more ambiguous, vague, nonoperational, and above all unprovable. Work that has been done in this vein is nevertheless comforting in that it suggests that the sociology of the state is inseparable from the study of social structures and that the notion of differentiation cannot hope to explain anything unless it is applied to a specific historical context and used in conjunction with other ideas that functionalist sociology continues to neglect.

Offe's hypothesis is supported, moreover, by the fact that the process of differentiation has certain latent but not-to-be-underestimated effects, which also seem to contribute to maintaining or strengthening the established social order. In the first place the separation of the public and private spheres and the identification of the latter with the sphere of relations based on contract inevitably leads to an individualization of social relations and thus to generalization of the market system. The market system, in turn, cannot but favor those groups that happen to possess the most resources and the largest amounts of "human capital." This again tends to cast doubt on the claim that the state is neutral and makes its decisions on the basis of universalistic criteria.[103] Furthermore, differentiation tends in large part to depoliticize the private sphere, which then becomes subject to the claim by those in possession of "technical" or "technocratic" skills that their domination is legitimate. This, as Habermas observes, tends to disguise certain aspects of state intervention or to make them appear neutral, thereby limiting public debate that might pose a challenge to the technical decisions made by the leadership.[104]

Taken together, these observations make it clear that the simple causal relationship that functionalists see between the social division of labor and the rise of the state needs to be modified in a number of respects. To begin with, it is clear that the explanatory variable is not differentiation in general but rather the specific mode of differentiation, which is determined by the precise historical context and related to the combined impact of economic transformations (such as the agricultural crisis of the Middle Ages and the rise of the market economy), sociopolitical transformations (such as the breakdown of traditional forms of authority), and international transformations (such as the formation of a world economic system). Beyond that, it seems that differentiation need not necessarily lead to the construction of a full-blown state but only to the emergence of a more or less autonomous and differentiated political center. Only certain modes of centralization have led to the formation of true states, and this has happened only in response to the simultaneous effects of dedifferentiation and epigenesis, two processes which are themselves responses to particular historical situations and which are determined in part by specific ways of achieving the social division of labor and of organizing political power as well as by resistance to change by traditional elements in the society, all of which takes place within a specific cultural context.

From the foregoing remarks three tentative conclusions may be drawn. First, the emergence of the state is influenced by many variables, which determine the nature of political development in each case in the context of a specific cultural code (to be discovered by analysis). Second, whereas sociology enables us to define the various ways in which state and society are interrelated and to identify the general factors that play an important role in the state-building process, it is up to historical analysis to identify the specific factors at work in any particular case and to explain how these factors relate to one another. Finally, notwithstanding our proposed revisions and criticisms, functionalist sociology is still capable of providing, if not an explanation of the origins of the state (the effort to do this seems to have ended in failure), then at least a reasonably useful description of its characteristic features. In particular, it has been shown that the true state (as distinguished from what is merely the center of a centralized political system) is one that has achieved a certain level of differentiation, autonomy, universality, and institutionalization. These features remain characteristic, even if their significance may not be as great as some writers have maintained. Limitations have been revealed not only by theoretical criticism but also in political practice, and it has been shown that all of the features named may coexist with dedifferentiation and epigenesis. What is more, these four characteristics may be put to various uses, not all of which can be regarded as purely rational goals.

Critique of One-dimensionality

Not only has functionalist sociology (until recently dominant in the field) given a simplistic account of the origins of the state, it has also been quick to regard the state as a universally valid political form suitable for all societies. Functionalists have thus denied that cultural diversity leaves room for more than one possible type of political organization. This position has in fact been reached in various ways. For the classical anthropologists, especially Lowie, the state is an elementary social fact common to all cultures. From this it follows that states exist in all societies, at least in embryonic form. Modernization theorists, on the other hand, regard the state as the superstructure of industrial society and therefore hold that it inevitably emerges in connection with social and economic development, wherever it occurs. For functionalist theorists, Parsons in particular, the state is the product of a unique and as it were "elect" culture, and the success of this mode of political organization, we are told, will lead to its being adopted in all parts of the world, thanks to the influence of the industrial revolution. Contemporary Marxist sociology is no different from the rest, for by directing attention exclusively to Marx the evolutionist, his followers tend to view the state as being related to a particular type of social formation, of universal significance in their view, and this leads them to believe that the structures of the state will inevitably gain in strength in all political societies, even if this situation is only temporary. Thus in each of the theoretical traditions mentioned, the state is seen as gaining universal ascendancy either as the result of a process of rationalization in the social system or as a phase of that process.

There are several weaknesses in this position. From a purely logical point of view, it is based on an oversimplified notion of rationality, which leads to the assumption that a political system based on the principle of rationality must necessarily be of the same form regardless of its cultural context. Against this view it may be suggested that rationalization, insofar as it is true that it plays a role in social development, should be thought of simply as a way of developing specific elements of a cultural tradition in a coherent and abstract way and of seeking to relate those elements to science and technology. With this idea in mind it becomes naïve and arbitrary to believe that rationalization, in the sense of rationalizing a tradition, can only follow the Western pattern and can only lead, in the political sphere, to unification of all cultures and traditions under the umbrella of the state. Sociological analysis might, on the other hand, be able to escape the impasse in which it finds itself if the order of the factors is reversed and state building is seen as just one among many possible forms of rationalization, which happens to have been the form that guided the development of a limited number of European societies during the early modern period.

Such a reversal would offer the additional advantage of filling in a gap in classical sociological theory by restoring to culture its proper role in the explanation of the rise of the state. It would make it possible to relate the rise of the state not only to the social division of labor, the power structure, or the condition of the social system but also to a specific cultural code within which the Christian religion, Roman law, and Greek philosophy could be seen to have played a key role in determining the specific pattern of political development in Europe.

With this sort of revision, sociological theory might find it possible to deal with problems that it has thus far approached in a very limited way. What forms other than the state may political modernization take? How can we explain the variety of ways in which states are organized? How can we account for the failure of societies in the third world to create viable states? On this last point, it is possible, even in the present state of our knowledge, to suggest that the crises experienced by political systems in Africa, Asia, and South America have to do not so much with the inadequacy of their governmental structures as with the unwise attempt to graft a formula for political rationalization derived from Western experience onto radically different cultural traditions. A far cry from any sort of natural growth process, state building in these societies has been burdened by the weight of traditional relations of dependence and by the myth of the universal state, which dominates the international order, as well as by the so-called "demonstration effect," which, if Gino Germani is correct, leads less developed societies to follow recipes that seem to have worked elsewhere in trying to resolve their own problems.[105]

The only way to confirm the foregoing hypotheses is by patient research into the cultural factors affecting the emergence of Western states and influencing their nature and characteristics. If culture is defined not in terms of cults and costumes but rather as a set of "structures of meaning whereby men give shape to their experience," and if one follows Geertz in thinking that the "political arena" is probably the place where these structures emerge most clearly,[106] then it is natural to argue that the crux of political change lies in giving shape to the encounter between tradition and innovation in economy, society, and politics. Political change, regardless of whether it takes place in early modern Europe or in the third world today, presupposes that some aspects of tradition will remain unchanged. What remains constant will of course vary from one culture to another, shaping the process of political centralization in ways peculiar to each particular culture.[107] It is thus possible to argue that what functionalists see as attributes of the modern nation-state in general are in fact partly determined by the particular cultural context in which the state first developed.

Let us first look at differentiation in this light. Shmuel Eisenstadt acknowledges in his most recent work that the capacity of a society to differentiate and to develop multiple centers of decision-making is a consequence of historical processes peculiar to the West, associated in particular with the aftermath of feudalism. He further admits that Eastern Europe has political structures just as centralized as those in Western Europe. But he claims that centralization in the East was not a way of compensating for social differentiation but rather a result of the prince's traditional monopoly of political power. Furthermore, claims to a monopoly of political power are being put forward today in social systems that were never feudal to any significant degree, that have had little experience of representative politics, and that exhibit a pyramidal social structure rather than a pluralistic class structure.[108] Much the same idea can be found in the work of historians like Otto Hintze, who emphasize the link between the formation of highly differentiated states of the type found in the West and the existence of a culture in which politics and religion are distinct and in which there is a powerful, decentralized aristocracy.[109] This line of argument fits in quite well with Clifford Geertz's detailed analysis of modernization in Indonesia. Geertz concludes that it makes no sense in the context of Indonesia's national political culture to try to account for the actions of the government in Djakarta in terms of its supposed function, namely, to coordinate the different aspects of public life in the country.[110] It does not follow from this that some modern industrial societies may not need a political center. But Geertz's analysis does suggest that neither the Western model of social differentiation nor the political structure to which it leads, in which the center plays a coordinating role, are necessarily compatible with political cultures found elsewhere in the modern world.

Much the same might be said of the notion of autonomy, which functionalists are wont to see as a universal characteristic of all modern social structures. As we saw earlier, the classical model is not entirely consistent on the subject of autonomy, in that not all European political systems developed truly autonomous bureaucracies. As a result, a distinction has had to be made between fully developed state systems and political systems of the type found in Great Britain, which though highly centralized have developed no more than limited forms of the state. The degree of bureaucratic autonomy varies even in fully developed states, however: in Germany, for example, it is easy to move back and forth between the political arena and the bureaucracy, whereas in the United States this is virtually impossible. One possible way of explaining this would be in terms of cultural differences related to the very different histories of the two societies. Germans very early learned to rely on government bureaucracy to protect their constitutional liberties, but Americans are still suspicious of their bureaucracy, whose image was tarnished during the colonial period when the administration served tyrannical ends.[111] On this view of the matter, the degree of autonomy in a political system is not to be seen as an independent variable but rather as a dependent variable that is in part culturally determined. Hence autonomy is no longer a characteristic feature of all modernized societies but rather an attribute that can in some contexts be put to use in achieving modernization.

Peter Nettl has shown that institutionalization is also related to culture. Two distinct types of political culture have served as the basis for modern political systems: Nettl refers to one of these as "constitutional" culture, defined as a culture in which the political system can act autonomously and tends to rely on normative mechanisms to cope with problems and crises, and to the other as "elitist" culture, in which social interaction takes precedence over institutional structures and political authority is bestowed largely on social and political elites, selected on the basis of either performance criteria or traditional criteria.[112] As "constitutional" cultures Nettl lists Germany and France and on dubious grounds adds the United States. Clearly, these are societies with modern states according to the narrow definition. The "elitist" type of culture is exemplified by Great Britain, to which Nettl adds, again dubiously, Russia. The political systems in these countries are not highly institutionalized or are institutionalized only in a symbolic sense, which leaves the "establishment" a wide latitude to act as it pleases. This typology, Nettl notes, is based in part on cultural traits, in that it takes account of the possible range of action orientations and modes of evaluation of social processes.[113]

The foregoing discussion suggests two possible avenues for further research. One would be to study the history of Western Europe in order to find out what economic, social, and political variables can be used to explain the formation of the nation-state as well as the degree to which the state has developed in different societies. Another would be to undertake a rigorous investigation of the way in which these variables interacted with a particular cultural code. This is important because it seems clear that the nature of this code will be crucial in determining how far political systems of a Western type can be transferred to modern third world societies.

Part Two

State, Society, and History

History has been combined with sociological analysis to show that modernization—or at any rate entry into the industrial age—is accompanied by a process that leads to the emergence of a political center.[1] To be sure, centralized political systems have been a feature not only of modern but also of many ancient or classical societies. The novelty of modern times is that exceptions to the law of centralization are no longer tolerated, the division of labor in modern society being such that none can escape the need for coordination through a centralized political structure or structures. But this is the only common feature of modern political systems, and as soon as the political sociologist begins to concern himself with history or simply with the empirical data he is forced to admit that political centralization may take many different forms and that the particular form that emerges in any given case is largely related to cultural and conjunctural factors: state-building is only one form of political centralization among others, and the models followed in building states vary widely from one society to the next. It has been said that the state[2] is the product of a specific historical process, that of Western Europe, and of a specific era, the Renaissance. What this historical observation suggests is that the rise of the state comes about primarily in response to a specific crisis situation in a given period and place, and, further, that there is no a priori reason to regard the state as a valid resolution of other kinds of crises, occurring in other times and places.

Accordingly, it is impossible to understand the rise of the state in Europe without a careful analysis of the circumstances attending the process of political centralization in the societies of the old continent, including the special circumstances surrounding the division of labor in each country of Europe. In this way it may become possible to view the state as an ideal type, an extreme solution of the problems faced by a number of European societies in which internal differentiation of the underlying social structures proved to be difficult to achieve. This view leads to the further hypothesis that the solution arrived at in each country was worked out in response not only to the needs of integration and coordination but also to the specific historical circumstances surrounding the centralization process as well as to the previously existing social and political structures and cultural traditions that made each society unique.

3   State,
Division of Labor,
and Capitalism

Most historians are accustomed to explaining the rise of the state in Europe by invoking socioeconomic changes that began in the late Middle Ages and continued for several centuries. As a result, the nature of social interaction was profoundly altered as specialized new tasks were created and the division of labor progressed. Historical analysis of particular regions has revealed this kind of pattern, and, as a way of introducing our subject, it is worth pausing for a moment to consider what the historians have found out. To take one notable example, Charles Tilly's detailed monograph on the Vendée in the period leading up to the French Revolution shows how traditional communal structures in the Loire Valley area of the province were destroyed by the gradual rise of a market economy and by the development of close ties between town and countryside as well as increasing specialization in economic life.[1] These socioeconomic changes had direct consequences in the political sphere: new structures developed to coordinate the diversified economic activities; a specialized political elite emerged; rural areas became increasingly dependent on emerging urban centers; and, last but not least, a slow process of differentiation gradually produced an autonomous political center, which was receptive to then current republican ideas and thus able to link the populace of the Loire Valley to the national political center in Paris.[2]

What makes Tilly's work even more noteworthy is that he has also succeeded in showing that in another part of the Vendée, the Mauges region, where economic development was late, sudden, and disorderly, the process was the reverse: rural communes tended to resist change by turning inward, the volume of trade grew little if at all, and progress in the social division of labor was slow.[3] Now, it was precisely this part of the Vendée that remained for the most part loyal to the king during the French Revolution, and that saw both the Chouan uprising, hostile to the Revolution, and the development of antirepublican ideas. Not only was this region politically reactionary, it was also stubbornly resistant to further centralization, the effect of which was to relegate the Mauges to peripheral status.[4] The contrast between the Mauges and Loire regions of the Vendée is a microcosm of France's difficulties in moving toward modernization. Hence the study of this period of French history can help to illustrate the difference between a full-fledged state and a mere centralized political system, a difference earlier encountered in our more theoretical discussion. More specifically, when we look at the process of centralization in the Loire region of the Vendée, we find that few problems were encountered and that centralization took place rapidly and without coercion. In the royalist Mauges area, however, there was considerable resistance to the kinds of social change that would have led to a more centralized system, and these changes proved difficult to effect. Because of this opposition, the central political institutions were radicalized and encouraged to develop authoritarian and bureaucratic characteristics. With further encouragement from the Revolution, what finally emerged was a state-centered political system. The consequences for sociological theory may be summarized as follows. The social division of labor seems to require the development of a political center; for a true state to emerge, however, something more is needed. In particular, the rise of the state is related to the way in which traditional society breaks down. In the case of the Vendée there was local resistance to change and to integration in new patterns of trade. In short, it is the conditions under which modern social formations supplant traditional social formations that influence the development of the state.[5]

With this hypothesis in mind, it becomes easier to understand why Eastern Europe followed a different course of modernization from that of Western Europe. Particularly in the southern reaches of the West there was strong solidarity among peasant communities, whereas in the East, as Robert Brenner has shown, the bonds uniting the peasantry were weak and there were virtually no autonomous village communities.[6] In these circumstances East European landowners were able to respond to the social and economic crisis by using force and coercion to restore control over the peasantry, whereas the attempt to do the same thing in Western Europe was doomed to failure and served only to radicalize social conflict to the point where the only possible recourse was to a centralized and authoritarian state. There is no denying the fact that the state first appeared in Western Europe. It is also true that east of the Elbe the institutionalization of servile relations served in many ways as a functional substitute for the state.

That there is a connection between state building and changes in the social structure is rather convincingly demonstrated by the foregoing interpretation of European history. This being the case, can we then go beyond Tilly to argue that the economy is the most important factor in causing this kind of political change? Is it true that the social changes associated with the rise of the state were themselves consequences of specific changes in the economy, particularly the development of mercantile capitalism toward the end of the Middle Ages? Immanuel Wallerstein, for one, does not hesitate to assert that it was precisely this economic revolution that was the leading factor in the rise of the state. He supports this contention by showing that the development of ocean trade gave rise to a worldwide capitalist market and thus to an international economic system whose ramifications stretched far beyond the tiny promontory on the Eurasian land mass that we know by the name of Europe. The center of the new economy shifted from time to time but soon came to rest in the northwestern corner of Europe, and from there central control was extended to dominate a periphery that stretched to the eastern and southern fringes of the old Continent.[7] The center (which consisted essentially of England and the northwestern quarter of continental Europe) was characterized by highly differentiated economic structures and by the rapid growth of mercantile capitalism. The only way for the center to develop economically was to exploit societies lying on its periphery. These peripheral societies served as a breadbasket for the more dynamic central societies. Economic activity on the periphery was confined to the sphere of agriculture, so that the peripheral societies could not follow the center's lead and take advantage of the recent changes in the world economy. Now Wallerstein argues that the only way for this system to perpetuate itself was for strong states to arise at its center while at the same time the emergence of strong states was being impeded on the periphery.[8] Looked at in this way, the absolutist state is merely the political form first assumed by the nascent capitalist system. The theory is that the state organized the social division of labor from which the most advanced societies were reaping the profits. No matter which version of the state we are talking about, Tudor or Bourbon, the reason for its rise is the same: the state was functional, it protected the new organization of the economy and the new social elites dependent on that organization, it hastened the shift from agriculture to industry, it fostered the search for new markets, and it assured control of the seas.[9] By contrast, on the periphery, Wallerstein argues, the absence of state structures was necessary in order to allow reproduction of the system of central domination and the perpetuation of a system of single-crop agriculture. Using the Polish example, Wallerstein shows how the spread of serfdom and the assumption of political responsibility by the landed aristocracy not only delayed the crystallization of the Polish political system around the power of the monarch but also encouraged the development of direct trade in grain with England and other states of the center.[10]

It is important, however, to understand that the birth of the state was not merely the *result* of the development of mercantile capitalism in Europe, as Wallerstein himself is forced to admit in the course of his argument. It is clear, in fact, that state structures were already in place when major crises shook the feudal economy in the fourteenth century, hence well before the opening of the seas and the attendant economic changes.[11] Wallerstein is even willing to agree with Edouard Perroy's contention that the origins of the state can be traced back to the thirteenth century.[12] Thus he admits that as early as 1250 the royal administration was clever enough to profit from the expansion of the rural economy and growth of the population so as to increase its tax revenues and amass resources from which it derived a great deal of power.[13] The state profited in equal meaure from the great crisis that developed in the following century, when falling seigneurial revenues forced it to engage for the first time in monetary manipulations on a large scale and when declining consumption led it to expand the scope of its activities and undertake what amounts to nothing less than an interventionist economic policy.[14] There is hardly any doubt, then, that the major transformations of the Renaissance period took place within a socio-political context that already featured an organized state as one of its key elements, and furthermore that this state had already had the experience of coping with a wide variety of economic structures and conjunctures and of doing so with some measure of autonomy.[15]

Having taken note of this important reservation to Wallerstein's line of argument, we are bound to admit that his work is unexceptionable when it comes to explaining the various ways in which state structures, where they formed, helped to consolidate the newly emerged system of mercantile capitalism. There is no denying that governments were able to protect and even to organize society in accordance with a number of the economic system's needs. It is equally certain that the development of a state bureaucracy and the establishment of a standing army required stepped-up efforts of production and extensive recourse to borrowing, as a result of which a banking system came into existence.[16] Corroborating this line of argument, Perry Anderson also shows how the formation of a uniform legal system, the lifting of certain barriers associated with the structure of feudal society, and the development of colonial enterprises produced similar effects.[17] Even more important, the very existence of the state as a mode of political organization within the new international economic system greatly stimulated the growth of trade. Because the territorial division of Europe tended toward the development of a number of nation-states rather than a single transnational empire, enterprises in the economic sphere were able to operate more autonomously and extend their activities beyond national boundaries and thus beyond the control of any political body.[18] Wallerstein alludes to this idea when he notes that the failure of the Spanish Armada and, with it, of the last dreams of European empire, was more important than any other material factor in the development of Western capitalism.[19] A related argument has been put forward by Victor Kiernan, who believes that the size of the nation-state was almost perfectly tailored to meet the needs created by the new social and economic situation: the states that developed in Europe were large enough to survive and yet small enough to allow the government to exert effective central control and coordination.[20]

Wallerstein carries this argument even further in the systematic exposition of his ideas. Not only was the state useful at the center of the new economic system, but, Wallerstein maintains, the failure of states to develop on the periphery was also functional in that it reproduced the relations of domination among the various European nations. Thus the late development of the Polish state can be explained in terms of the same factors that account for the early development of Western European states.[21] Russia is no exception: the attempts to establish a state there as early as the sixteenth century under Ivan the Terrible, for example, were merely a part of a brief effort to establish Russian autonomy vis-à-vis the nascent Western economy. When the Romanovs came to power, they abandoned these attempts, since they hoped to integrate the empire of the tsars into the European economic system as a peripheral agricultural power. The effect of this was to accentuate the predominance of the aristocracy and ultimately to create a political system which, while centralized, lacked any semblance of an autonomous bureaucracy of the sort that plays such an important role in our model of the state.[22]

Although study of these various transformations reveals that the existence of a rather close functional tie between economic change and state building is highly likely, reality is nevertheless more complicated than a quick glance at this model would suggest. To begin with, the state is not limited to its purely functional role, as Wallerstein himself shows. Furthermore, even from a functionalist standpoint, state building cannot be understood primarily in terms of its contributions to the nascent capitalist economic system. Although states were equipped with means of responding to the economic convulsions associated with the birth of capitalism, their reason for doing so, it should be remembered, often had to do with their need to further their own inherent political interests. Philip the Fair's monetary policy was determined primarily by military requirements, whereas the aim of his successors was chiefly to finance a growing bureaucracy.[23] What is more, as the state grew in France, it adopted an interventionist policy with regard to industry that not only failed to serve the interests of the emerging economic elites but actually worked primarily to make the productive apparatus dependent on the state or at any rate subject to its control.[24] Even before interventionist policies were institutionalized under Colbert, the absolute monarchy maintained tight control over the manufacture of gunpowder and saltpeter for military purposes. Still earlier, the Valois kings had taken over the mines, not only to secure a new source of revenue but also to limit the growth of an economic power that threatened the state's monopoly of domination: this seems the best way to explain why a bureaucratic apparatus was established during the fifteenth century for the purpose of administering French mines under the supervision of *surintendants* appointed by the central authorities.[25]

Even if we look at the state in terms of its relation to civil society, we find that its actions were apparently intended mainly to protect a crisis-ridden feudal and agricultural society and to help it adapt to change rather than to defend the new capitalist elite.[26] To the extent that the Tudor and Stuart political system possessed adequate organizational capacities, it was concerned more with impeding enclosure than with cementing an alliance between the aristocracy and the industrial bourgeoisie. Similarly, in France it can hardly be denied that the burgeoning bureaucracy was most often called upon to deal with social conflict or impending famine and to perpetuate an economy based largely on land and ground rent. Thus the state did not respond to the tensions in civil society in the manner suggested by Wallerstein. Rather, it acted as though its goal was to prevent economic change from causing intolerably violent or chaotic upheaval. Indeed, it was to this end that the absolute monarchy later intervened in the economy in order to perpetuate the existence of the old feudal class and indeed to make that class the main beneficiary of changes in the economy.[27]

In view of the defects pointed out above, Wallerstein's rather summary argument seems somewhat less persuasive than the more subtle reasoning of Perry Anderson, who sees the state—at least in its beginnings—as the consequence of a reallocation of the resources of feudal society in response first to a crisis within that society and later to the rise of a market economy.[28] This kind of argument is useful for moving from a functionalist to a genetic view of the state. Its fundamental assumption is that states were most likely to develop in societies that encountered difficulties in moving from the old to the new division of labor, whether because of social opposition to change or because of problems of a technological or political order.

In support of this assumption, it is worth noting that it is indeed true that differentiated state structures were less likely to develop in societies that adapted easily to the new world economy and that were quicker than their neighbors to profit from the transition. Thus the Netherlands, at the very center of the early modern economy, never required an authoritarian political structure (of the type described by Wallerstein) to coordinate its economic activities. The country was actually a constitutional state run by an oligarchy of businessmen whose autonomy was relatively limited. It is legitimate to ask to what extent the limited development of the Dutch state was due precisely to the ease of transition from a rural economy to an advanced form of market economy.[29] Similarly, in England the absolutist phase was exceptionally brief: "the Tudor state," on which much of Wallerstein's model is based,[30] did result in a strengthening of executive power and extensive recruitment of civil servants by the central government. The development of Tudor political structures was nevertheless less extensive than the corresponding development in France. Furthermore, not even at the height of Henry VIII's reign was there sufficient development of either the fiscal administration or the military to allow us to speak of a true state. Born early and with relative ease, English capitalism in fact helped to perpetuate weak state structures and a disinclination to intervene in the economy, so that civil society was left to organize on its own without interference by the prince. Contemporary philosophical literature, notably the work of Locke, reflects this pattern of development. If there was a push toward centralization in the sixteenth and seventeenth century, it was in response to ephemeral circumstances and not a consequence of the structure of English society or the world economy.[31]

Furthermore, Wallerstein is forced to modify his argument somewhat when he comes to consider the case of France, where he notes that the rapid rise of absolutism had to do not so much with the development of new economic networks in Flanders and the Ile-de-France as with the need to reconcile the growing volume of trade with the persistence of an agriculturally based economy in the provinces south of the Loire.[32] Wallerstein's argument thus furnishes magesterial confirmation of our contention that societies in which economic growth is unproblematical are likely to be able to get along without a state, and, conversely, that history shows that states take hold not whereever capitalism emerges but rather where they are needed to cope with the social crises that sometimes accompany the growth of a capitalist economy. The difference between the two positions may seem slight, but it can be of great importance, particularly since too much development of the state can impose costs so high as to impede the development of capitalism. In fact, many historians argue that the new economic elites in England were considerably aided by the weakness of the state and the modesty of public expenditure, which made for a reduced fiscal burden on the economy.[33]

To some extent we share the view of a number of authors who, in direct contrast to Wallerstein, have argued that the only infrastructural factor that might plausibly have played a role in the formation of the state is that of economic backwardness, if for no other reason than that backwardness may result in a stiffening of the resistance to changes in traditional social structures. Such at any rate is the conclusion reached by Alexander Gerschenkron (who studied a much later period than Wallerstein). Gerschenkron sees late industrialization as a possible explanation of the peculiar patterns of development not only in France but even more in Germany and Russia.[34] Breaking sharply with classical Marxist tenets (which Wallerstein adopts without the least criticism), Gerschenkron cogently demonstrates that the primitive accumulation model covers only the one case of English industrialization, and furthermore that the later economic development occurs, the more brutal and costly it is in social terms, since late development requires specialized institutions for the accumulation of capital and the coordination and planning of economic activity. This accounts for the role played by investment banks in France, Germany, and Austria, and for the differences between the industrialization process in those countries and the English pattern of industrialization, of which the characteristic features were decentralization, gradualism, and incorporation of the agricultural economy. These differences have clear political implications: in England, where development was based on the model of primitive accumulation, the key economic functions were carried out by the existing social structure and this reduced the power of the central government, whereas in France and Germany and above all in Russia the need to amass large amounts of capital in a short period of time turned governments into nothing less than economic development agencies and resulted in the attribution of extensive powers to the state. Using the example of Russia, Gerschenkron shows how the industrial takeoff of the Tsarist empire was accomplished by state agencies, which not only established needed infrastructure and banking institutions but also worked to encourage investment via fiscal policy.[35]

Most historical treatments of industrialization confirm and even amplify Gerschenkron's conclusions, drawing an even more radical distinction between the fundamentally individualistic English model and most continental models, in which the state was truly the driving force in building an industrialized economy. In this respect there is truly impressive continuity in the transition from Colbertian mercantilism and the establishment of state-run royal manufactories[36] to the elaboration of a "national policy for the encouragement of industry" under Napoleon I[37] to the policies inspired by the Saint-Simonians under Napoleon III. There is an equally clear progression in Prussia from Frederick the Great's policy of public aid and investment benefiting textile and chemical factories[38] to the economic role of the *Steuerräte* and *Fabrikinspektoren* and the Bismarckian policy of economic and industrial expansion. The same could be said of Belgium and, at a later date, of Italy.

The circumstances surrounding the construction of the railroads—truly the backbone of an industrial economy—add further confirmation, if confirmation is needed, of the foregoing observations. The railroad construction that followed the Industrial Revolution in England was a private affair, whereas in France the state worked hand in hand with private companies. In Germany certain parts of the rail system were built entirely on state initiative, and in Belgium the government had a complete monopoly of rail construction.[39]

Gerschenkron is mistaken, however, in thinking that the different patterns of industrialization correlate exclusively with the degree of economic backwardness. In fact, in all the societies that Gerschenkron considers there was a long-standing tradition of state intervention. Hence it would seem more appropriate to relate the extent of state development to such factors as resistance to change, limited capacities of coordination, and fragmentation of legal and political systems, all of which are found to one degree or another in many preindustrial social formations. Taken together, it seems likely that these factors can account for the propensity of the state to intervene in the economy (as well as for the targets and conservative aims of such intervention) and even for economic backwardness itself. The combination of these factors leads to an "accelerator effect" relating industrialization and *étatisation:* economic action by the government becomes increasingly necessary in order to overcome the cumulative effects of backwardness and to cope with international competition as well as to create a market by artificial means.

To sum up then, there is a close and suggestive relationship between the formation of a political center and the gradual extension of the social division of labor: with this proposition no one will quarrel. Nor will anyone object to the contention that in this respect the economic factor plays an important role: the decline of agriculture followed by the slow rise of a market economy certainly contributed to social differentiation and to the emergence of political structures to coordinate newly diversified economic activities. Where Wallerstein and other overly "economistic" theorists go wrong, we think, is in their attempt to infer from this evidence the truth of a far more dubious proposition: because the rise of capitalism accelerates the transformation of the economy and leads to further division of labor, they argue, it must inevitably give rise to "complete" political centralization, or, in other words, it must inevitably lead to the formation of a state. This conclusion is simplistic for two reasons: first, it is based on the assumption that the economy alone determines how labor is divided within a society, and second, it takes for granted the assertion that society cannot "function" without the state. Thus social inertia is completely discounted, and so are the most glaring sorts of differences between one society and another: differences relating to the division of labor, to resistance to change, and to social tension, which determine whether or not centralization will lead to authoritarianism and whether or not the end result will be a true state or something else.

What Wallerstein neglects to point out is the fact that the "modern world system" was composed of a number of very different societies, each of which was more or less prone to develop a state independent of its position of dependence or level of development. Well before the advent of the modern economic system, serfdom had spread throughout Eastern Europe because the social formation in existence there tolerated private authority relations. This impeded state building in Eastern Europe for a time and influenced the state-building process when it finally did occur.[40] By contrast, the societies that Wallerstein describes as "semiperipheral" were strongly marked by the persistence of communal social relations—often of a feudal sort—and by strong resistance to change in rural social structures, which in large part accounts for the emergence in these societies of particularly highly structured states. These societies are to be contrasted with Great Britain, for example, where social relations became highly individualized at a very early date.

A few centuries later these patterns of development exerted an influence on the political strategy adopted by the dominated classes. It is obvious, for example, that differences in the developmental patterns of England and France affected the circumstances surrounding the birth of workers' movements in the two countries. In this regard it is significant that French socialism always had to define itself and organize its followers in a situation marked by the existence of a powerful state and by the conviction that proletarian victory could only come about after the government had been taken over by the workers. This was a tenet shared by both Guesdistes and revolutionary syndicalists, though the two groups interpreted the point in different ways. The Guesdistes used it to play down the importance of agitation for higher wages and better working conditions and to play up the omnipotent role of the party, while the revolutionary syndicalists emphasized the general strike as a way of overcoming the power of the state.[41] Thus the two major influences on contemporary French socialism agreed that political action should take priority over the corporate interests of labor and that the struggles of the workers should be waged not on the terrain of civil society but rather in the political arena.[42] People subject to both influences were motivated by a desire to mobilize against the capitalist state but differed mainly over the question of what tactics would lead most quickly to a revolutionary situation.[43] It should therefore come as no surprise that, once the strategy of the general strike had failed, the French workers' movement reconstituted itself on a partisan political basis, emphasizing the action of an avant-garde and the subordination of union to party (though of course this relationship has often been subject to various interpretation). If we compare state-labor relations in France with state-labor relations in other countries, the similarities and differences speak for themselves. Debates on this issue in Spain and Italy were virtually the same as those in France.[44] In Germany we see the first example of a country in which the working class established a well-organized, mass-based political party and forced the unions to tailor their actions to fit in with party strategy.[45] Although the success of the

German Social Democratic Party exposed it to some degree to reformist influences, it is easy to see why the labor movements in all these countries were in general so susceptible to Leninist influence and receptive to the Communist model, since they chose to base their tactics on party politics and to focus exclusively on the problem of the "bourgeois state."

By contrast, the limited development of the state in England was partly responsible for the fact that the labor movement that developed there was interested more in shop-floor and corporatist issues than in politics or revolution. When the comparison is carried out at this level, the "trade union model" is seen to be a perfectly logical development in a civil society with considerable capacities for self-organization. It is thus easy to understand why, in these circumstances, British trade unionism should have moved on, after conducting strikes for higher wages and better working conditions, to establish and run the Labour Party, which at least as far as structure is concerned has always been a mere parliamentary extension of the Trades Union Council (TUC).[46] In contrast to what we find in French labor history, English trade unions very quickly developed into institutionalized components of civil society. We see this quite clearly in the collective bargaining agreements reached early in the century, in which the government played no part, as well as in the TUC's active participation in the elaboration of a British economic plan.[47] Furthermore, not only do the unions dominate the party (the exact opposite of the situation on the Continent), but they have never been at the center of political debate or an important political issue as in France and Italy. This discussion shows convincingly, we think, that the state plays an important role in determining how the labor movement will organize and what strategies it will adopt. This in turn sheds additional light on the nature of the state's autonomy.

4   State and Social Structure

If it is true that the state arose in answer to crises that threatened the disintegration of certain societies in Europe, crises that basically involved resistance to change in social formations based on the community, then there is reason to believe that in order to explain the state's rise we must look to the feudal past. This is the fundamental assumption on which Perry Anderson has based his work.[1]

It is clear that the inherent logic of the feudal system was such as to make a particularly thorough monopolization of political power quite likely to occur, just as economic competition among small production units is likely to lead to the triumph of one of them over the rest and thus to the emergence of a monopoly. Developing this comparison still further, Norbert Elias astutely points out that feudal society was characterized by considerable confusion of roles: the lord wielded both political power and economic power, so that it was quite natural to use the sword to acquire new wealth, thereby giving rise to permanent conflict and competition between geographical regions.[2] A further stimulus to continual armed conflict was the fact that each participant felt a constant need to exert control over an ever wider area in order to prevent neighboring territories from falling into the hands of a more powerful antagonist.[3] With this mechanism in mind we can see how victory after victory led, by the end of the Middle Ages, to a situation in which a few lords controlled territories large enough and sufficiently centralized to be regarded as small states. Historically this was the last step prior to the integration of these territories into national units with safe, defendable boundaries.[4] While the feudal system may well have been stable in conditions of a closed economy, in other circumstances it turned out to harbor a great deal of self-destructive energy which led to the emergence of a highly centralized, not to say authoritarian, political system that went a long way toward institutionalizing the political power it monopolized.

The state was not simply a product of the feudal system, however. Its origins are also bound up with the way in which feudalism was related to the technological and economic context of the late Middle Ages. At that time the nature of warfare was profoundly altered by the use of artillery and infantry, which led to a considerable decline in the importance of the fortified castle and gave considerable new importance to the nonaristocratic social groups responsible for carrying out recently developed military functions.[5] This gradual loss by the aristocracy of one of its key sources of power was combined with the effects of a growing money economy, which had a particularly strong impact on the feudal system, shaking the very principles of its organization by weakening the tie of peasant to lord and counterbalancing aristocratic domination with the weight of a newly arisen bourgeoisie. All these factors contributed to the disintegration of civil society under feudalism by thwarting the operation of its reproductive mechanisms and cutting the ground out from under the lords, who had previously had almost exclusive control over all political power. Countries like England, where the influence of feudalism was relatively slight, were able to respond to the first challenges of modernization merely by making minor adjustments in their social structure and strengthening the ability of the central government to carry out functions for which it had already assumed responsibility. By contrast, societies in which the influence of the feudal past was strong were unable to move into the modern era thanks to the efforts of civil society alone. In order to maintain social integration these societies were forced to set up autonomous political systems that were sufficiently differentiated from the rest of society and sufficiently institutionalized to compensate for the disabilities of civil society and to overcome resistance to change on the part of those social actors who stood to lose political prerogatives that they had long held. Thus it would seem that social innovation was necessary to establish states in societies where the feudal influence was strong, because of the peculiar way in which these societies responded to modernization.

The growing money economy threatened to destroy serfdom and thus to undermine the feudal mode of production, which was based on political and economic coercion to extract surplus value from the peasants who cultivated the land of the manors.[6] In the West these challenges to feudalism were aggravated by the fact that, whenever the lords attempted to reestablish their seigneurial rights, they encountered strong community resistance. This resistance unified rebel peasants and created a situation in which there was a danger that the rural population would flee the countryside and flock to the cities.[7] Once the usual political and legal forms of coercion ceased to be effective at the village level, the traditional social mechanisms tended to be displaced by state institutions, as is shown by the rapid penetration of royal bailiffs and officials into the areas of agricultural organization and control of the rural work force, in addition to which the government took steps to reduce peasant migration into the towns.[8]

It is beyond doubt that these developments were accelerated by the actions of the urban bourgeoisie, which in this and other respects reaped the benefits of the growing money economy. The position of the bourgeoisie in feudal society was quite novel, and this fact goes a long way toward explaining certain other peculiar aspects of the development of the state. In the first place, because the feudal system was characterized by the dispersion of sovereignty, cities were able to develop as autonomous entities in the interstices between the territory of one lord and that of another and thus generally beyond the control of the aristocracy.[9] Cities of this type are to be distinguished not only from Italian cities in which the landed aristocracy resided and which controlled the surrounding countryside, but also from the English towns, which in a relatively centralized context were more closely tied to the royal authorities.[10] Furthermore, the medieval city was a direct legacy of the Roman Empire and as such the repository of a juridical tradition that facilitated the task of institutionalizing property relations, encouraged the growth of an economy based on trade, and laid the groundwork for the formation of a centralized political system based on public law.[11]

Responding to the social and political crisis afflicting feudal society, the urban bourgeoisie contributed both directly and indirectly to the construction of the state. The mere existence of the bourgeoisie prevented the lords in the West from dealing with the peasantry in the same manner as the lords in the East, where the aristocratic response was to reimpose serfdom.[12] Furthermore, by asserting itself as a potential rival of the aristocracy, the bourgeoisie helped to undermine the political and social institutions on which feudalism was based. As a result there was a demand for the creation of a substitute form of state that would be able to assume control over the administration of the towns, the courts, and finances and to organize industry and commerce. These were the goals that guided the work of royal officials from the fifteenth century on.[13] The expanding monarchy established a close relationship with the urban bourgeoisie by using its members as agents and by setting up royal courts in the cities.

When we look at the state in terms of its functional role, however, it is important to note that, although the newborn state did strip the aristocracy of some of its political powers, it nevertheless tended to defend crucial social and economic privileges of the Second Order.[14] In the first place it protected private property. In fact private property was first given formal legal status during the period when the absolutist state was on the rise. Furthermore, the state erected a police apparatus equipped to put down any peasant protest or revolutionary aspirations. Last but not least, the central authorities established a system of taxation that exempted the nobility almost entirely and made it possible to reproduce the feudal mode of extracting profit on a national scale. It is difficult, however, to accept Anderson's view that the absolutist state was a mere instrument of the aristocracy. More cautiously, it may be observed that the states that came into being in this period by expelling the lords from the political arena, developing autonomous structures of government, and intervening in the economy often for reasons of their own— these states had no choice but to strike some kind of *compromise* with a civil society that was still largely dominated by the aristocracy in terms of both prestige and wealth and that was far less affected than some have maintained by supposed economic rivalry between the aristocracy and the bourgeoisie. The bourgeoisie of the Ancien Régime was profoundly influenced by the example of the aristocracy, and its motives were more social than they were capitalist. Furthermore, the bourgeoisie's economic aspirations centered on local commerce more than international trade and were well suited to a predominantly rural economy and to a state that was always in need of money to borrow. The fledgling state did indeed sanction a new political order, alter social practice, and shape new class strategies, but it did not seek to bring about any far-reaching changes in the system of social and economic domination, which was basically beneficial to the rural aristocracy and which, by helping to restrict the growth of a liberal market economy and system of industry, tended to lend still further strength to the state.[15] Here we find fresh confirmation of the correlation between the development of the state and industrial backwardness.

In sum, what we have found is that it was the *political* crisis of the feudal system that shaped the state as a specific form of political centralization. It seems clear that the state arose in response to two kinds of dysfunctions in what was a specifically European type of social order: one kind of dysfunction was connected with the extreme dispersion of sovereignty and with the identification of political, economic, and legal functions at the molecular level of society, i.e., the level of the *seigneurie,* while the other kind of dysfunction was related to the rigidity, not to say petrifaction, of the feudal social formation, which was unable either to adapt to the new division of labor in the absence of authoritarian forms of coordination or to maintain itself as such in the face of changes in the environment.[16] The state, therefore, is primarily the postfeudal version of a universal process of centralization of political structures: hence the states that arose in this period were much less sharply defined in northern societies in which the influence of Germanic tradition was strong and which did not experience the same degree of fragmentation of sovereignty during the medieval period as did the Mediterranean societies influenced primarily by Roman tradition, which were able to achieve stability quite early by building on the model of the city-state.[17]

On the basis of the foregoing discussion it is easy to see how the English monarchy was able to establish a political center very quickly without having to rely on an authoritarian bureaucracy, given that there was no need to subdue the aristocracy, which in any case was relatively uninfluenced by feudalism and unconcerned about achieving autonomy. In fact, the English aristocracy was more interested in exerting some control over the king than in challenging the legitimacy of royal institutions. England is thus in many respects typical of the kind of society that proved capable of developing a political center quite early and without major difficulty. This was possible in England (where a political center actually emerged as early as the ninth or tenth century) thanks to a very old tradition of representative government balanced by society's willingness to recognize the sovereignty of the monarch, who as early as the eleventh century accepted oaths of allegiance directly from all his subjects, without regard to the feudal hierarchy.[18] Because English society had never suffered from the rigidity or fragmentation associated with feudalism, it was able to achieve the centralization required by the socioeconomic changes of the early modern period without breaking with its past political tradition. This in turn explains why England was able to modernize without differentiating political from social roles or developing a state to anything like the degree we find in France, for example. It also explains why the English aristocracy was quick to assume the job of representing the royal administration and courts locally. It accounts for the fact that royal officials were for a long time volunteer public servants who belonged to the economic elites and, further, for the fact that the English Parliament (unlike the Paris *Parlement* in so many ways) not only represented the economic interests of an aristocracy allied with the bourgeoisie and involved in commerce but also served those interests in a direct political way.[19] With this in mind it is easy to understand why industry was so quick to develop in England and why the monarchy's attempts to intervene in the economy failed as well as why the royal government met with defeat at the hands of Parliament and the economic elites when it attempted to establish a bureaucratic state on the continental model. These different patterns of development are so important that one can only regret that Anderson, failing to follow the logic of his argument out to the end or even to make that logic explicit, settles for lumping all the various political systems of Europe together under the head "the absolutist state."

The hypothesis that the pattern of development makes a difference helps us to understand the peculiar features of the growth of the state in France. As Joseph Strayer has noticed, the state first arose in France in response to the need to establish or restore order in the country, which resulted in the establishment of judicial, administrative, and financial structures long before there was a diplomatic corps or an army.[20] Thus the first royal officials played the role of arbitrators, and they turned over a part of the income they earned in this way to the royal treasury; this is apparently why there was for a time so much confusion between the role of judge and that of fiscal agent of the king. Only gradually did tax officials gain autonomy from the courts, as state institutions became differentiated from one another and acquired the whole range of political responsibilities, domestic and foreign, characteristic of the modern nation-state.[21]

Finally, it is clear that the specific modalities of the modernization process influenced the development of the state along "pluralist" lines, allowing for more or less representation of peripheral interests. Because Western states generally developed in response to a fragmentation of sovereignty, the nature of traditional representative institutions is a factor that must be considered.[22] Furthermore, in order to integrate the feudal aristocracy into a new unified political structure, lords who stood to lose political power at the manorial level had to be compensated in some way, and this led, in France at any rate, to the formation of a judicial aristocracy in *parlement* and the other royal courts. Originally a center of resistance to change and a platform for social protest, the French *parlements* reflected the hierarchical and segmental structure of a civil society that was incapable of directly discharging its political responsibilities. The *parlements* long harbored seditious factions and at times served as "intermediary" bodies [in Montesquieu's sense] before belatedly laying claim to the status of representative institutions. In this sense, the Paris *parlement,* like other, similar bodies in other societies with strong states, is to be contrasted with the English *parliament* [the similarity of terminology is deceptive], which developed much earlier as a central governmental body. It is of course true that European political development has in many ways been associated with the rise of parliamentary institutions, and this may go some way toward explaining why even authoritarian or absolutist states, unable in general to rule despotically for very long, have been forced to depict themselves as pluralistic regimes carrying on the feudal tradition.

Logical as the foregoing historical sketch may be, its explanatory value will remain limited until we can explain what aspects of Western European tradition made for this kind of resoluton of the crisis of feudalism rather than some other outcome. It is to this task that we shall now turn our attention.

5   State, Culture, and the Emergence of the Political System

As the product of a specific, determinate social forma-
tion, the nation-state naturally took shape as a form of political organization that bore the stamp of a certain culture, the importance of which
should not be underestimated. As many sociologists and historians have
pointed out, more than one form of political organization could con-
ceivably have arisen at the end of the Middle Ages in response to the
crisis of feudal society. No matter how strict prevailing social and economic constraints may have been, infrastructural factors alone cannot
account for all the characteristic features of the type of state that was
"invented" in Europe during the Renaissance. If it was the social processes described above that led to this invention, it was the cultures of
Western Europe that governed the actual creation of the state as a real
entity. What these Western cultural models suggested was that the best
way to resolve conflicts and reduce tension was for society to develop
a distinct and autonomous political system.

The emergence of a distinct political system is most obvious when
we look at the relations that existed previously between religion and
politics. It is beyond doubt that Christianity played a major role in the
"invention" of the state and in the state-building process. The role of
Christianity became particularly important as the Church increasingly
asserted its autonomy in the spiritual domain, thereby laying down a
negative definition, as it were, of a temporal domain within which the
political system was left to develop its own legitimating criteria and
modes of operation.

Of course the separation of church and state did not come about all
at once: until the beginning of the second millennium religious and
political affairs were confounded with one another, with the clergy
occupying high positions in government and princes exercising the right
to name bishops and even to exert influence over the election of the
pope.[1] As Weber observed, however, even at this early date the Church
helped to shape the model on which the organization of future states

would be based in a number of respects. In the first place, it had perfected a unique and novel technique of government. Second, it had set
an example of hierarchical and bureaucratic forms of organization. And
finally, as Strayer points out, it had done much to propound a theory
of sovereignty, a theory that happened to be used in this particular case
to legitimate the authority of the pope as the head of a centralized
organization claiming a monopoly over certain kinds of power.[2]

But the Church's most direct influence on the state-building process
stemmed from the Gregorian reforms and the investiture conflict. These
episodes in the history of Christianity marked the real beginnings of the
separation of the spiritual from the temporal, reflecting the Church's
claim to full autonomy of action in the spiritual domain and its denial
of the right of princes and emperors to meddle in its affairs. Thus as
early as the eleventh century the papacy was in a position to claim a
monopoly of power in the spiritual domain and to strip the Christian
princes of all their religious prerogatives. This unprecedented event in
the history of civilization made plausible the idea of a self-organized
Church separated from the rest of society, the counterpart of which
was the concept of the state, which was seen as the necessary result of
a complete separation of the political system from the religious or cultural system.[3] The attendant realignment of political structures very
likely put an end to all imperial designs in Europe, because the basis
of European unity, which to some extent remained intact as long as
princely power was closely bound up with the symbolism of Christianity, was undermined once mere political authority became its only support. Moreover, this change probably accounts for the failure of the
Holy Roman Empire and for the gradual rise of nationalist sentiment.

The separation of religion and politics did not come about solely
because of circumstantial rivalries among ruling cliques. It corresponds
to certain fundamental tenets of Christian philosophy and theology.
From the first, Christianity insisted on distinguishing between what
belonged to "Caesar" and what belonged to God, between the "City of
Men," which can properly be established on earth, and the "City of God,"
which belongs to a supernatural world to come. It should be noted, however, that these distinctions are not found in all varieties of Christianity.
As heir to Byzantine tradition, the Eastern Orthodox Church has more
or less repudiated the distinctions in question, because it holds that the
emperor is God's representative on earth and that the temporal powers
are responsible for the protection of church and clergy, which are in fact
subordinate to the earthly ruler. Thus there is no basis for distinguishing

between the political powers and the sociocultural institutions. It is easy to see, then, why this model proved unsuitable for constructing a state.[4]

The Roman Catholic Church, on the other hand, confronted a temporal power that was far less potent and in fact on the verge of disintegration. Hence it had no difficulty promulgating the doctrine put forth by Saint Gelasius in the fifth century, that there is a necessary distinction between the power of the pope or *auctoritas,* which proceeds directly from Christ, and the power of the king or *potestas,* which is limited to the administration of earthly affairs.[5] This very clear separation of two domains and two powers undoubtedly served as a basis for the idea of an autonomous and specialized state distinct from civil society. It was reinforced and expanded in later years as a result of the growth and consolidation of the religious bureaucracy, the effect of which was inevitably to put pressure on states to organize in their own sphere of action and establish a stronger state presence in the midst of civil society. In this regard the later tendency toward secularization and the establishment of public schools can be viewed as the logical culmination of characteristics implicit in the state at its inception, indicative of the degree to which the expansion of the state, the rise of state bureaucracies, and the growth of state intervention are bound up with the influence of Catholicism.

The effects of this phenomenon were far less pronounced in societies that were exposed to the Reformation, however. The reformed churches contributed to a reduction of religious bureaucracy, favored increasingly individualized forms of worship, and broke all ties with Rome. As a result they soon found themselves serving their princes by helping to foster national sentiments and yet did not threaten the princely power by establishing a rival bureaucracy. This is probably the reason why the Protestant societies of Northern Europe generally developed political systems which, while centralized and legitimated on "rational-legal" grounds, were nevertheless less complex and extensive than the political systems that developed in countries lying to their south.[6] Notwithstanding Rokkan's pertinent remarks concerning the way in which the reformed churches helped to achieve national integration, there is no escaping the conclusion that Protestantism contributed to limiting the growth of the state. Thus the most highly developed forms of the state are primarily associated with Catholic cultures.

It is probably at this level of historical inquiry that sociological work based on the paradigm of differentiation is most ambiguous. As a product of the thorough separation of temporal and spiritual power en-

couraged by the culture of Catholicism, the legal, secular, and bureaucratic states that developed in the societies of southwestern Europe
came to wield supreme and independent sovereign power. These states
were subsequently able to promote economic development and, by
adopting interventionist, mercantilist economic policies, succeeded
either in combining the economic and political systems or in establishing
a close relationship between the two. In Protestant societies, on the
other hand, the political system is organically linked to religion and thus
directly dependent on the order of civil society itself, so that development of the state is limited and the boundary between the market and
politics is scrupulously respected. In Catholic societies the state establishes itself not as the culmination of a universal process of differentiation
but as the outcome of one particular mode of differentiation, wherein
the attempt to establish a radical distinction between the spiritual and
the temporal, the civil and the political, has led to an overestimation of
the importance of the political system, upon which legitimate authority
has been conferred to act as an autonomous and sovereign power.

Protestant tradition has by contrast modified and even rejected the
idea of differentiating between the political and the religious. What has
emerged instead in Protestant societies is a horizontal type of differentiation in which the emphasis is placed on individual liberty and the
division of labor—and hence on industrial enterprise—as factors favoring
social integration. At this stage of the argument various tendencies within
the Reformation need to be distinguished. To begin with, there is the
tendency that led to Anglicanism, by no means the least ambiguous version of Protestantism: while Anglicans hold that the religious and political domains are inseparable, they do so only in order to strengthen
their assertion that the terrestrial order is unified and that Church and
Crown, while distinct in function, are inseparable in substance and subject to the same law, which cannot be the law of Christ since that law is
applicable only to the realm of transcendence.[7] No doubt it was originally the intention of the monarch to use this doctrine to secure new
sources of power for himself, and he might have done so had the terrestrial order not been seen, in perfect harmony with the English model of
development, as the product of the traditions that governed civil society.
It is enough to read Richard Hooker to understand that in Anglican
doctrine the political order is based chiefly on parliament and on the
absence of a secular power, hence on the omnipotence of civil society.[8]

Puritanism, on the other hand, combined the temporal and spiritual
powers by identifying the City of Men with the City of God: the political order, in which coercion plays a role, is purely an affair of man and

as such destined to disappear as an independent entity in the course of reform. The administration of things as well as men is thus directly subject to the divine law. Although Cartwright does not challenge either the common law or the institutions of the Crown, it is clear that in his eyes the idea of a just state makes no sense unless the state is a supreme and sovereign power and the political system is merely an instrument for enforcing the commandments of religion, in particular those commandments that call for individual effort, personal reflection, and free choice.[9]

Of course the Calvinist view could be embodied in various concrete constitutional forms. Where reform emerged triumphant, the established order could rapidly develop into a quasi-dictatorial theocracy. Elsewhere, where Protestant thinking flourished in the context of a parliamentary opposition, as in Tudor and Stuart England, it could act as a liberalizing, individualistic influence. In places where the entire population adhered to the same Protestant sect, as in Massachusetts, religious ideas could govern economic and social as well as political life.[10] In any case, regardless of the surrounding circumstances, Protestantism invariably challenged the very idea of a sovereign state distinct from civil society, thereby establishing a line of political thinking at odds with Catholic ideas on the subject. In the Protestant version the role of differentiation was different, in that it was directed more toward the establishment of a market economy than toward institutionalization of the state.

When we look at the relations between the political system and the structure of the family, we find the same logic of separation at work. In the Middle Ages the nuclear family was the predominant form in Western Europe, and there were no strict blood ties linking lord and peasant. This foreshadowed the later individualization of social relations and dissociation of political responsibilities from the kinship system. Even before the rise of the state, European society was distinguished by a rather sharp differentiation between the sphere of the family and the sphere of politics, and this cleared the way for the centralization and monopolization of political functions. Conditions in Europe were considerably more favorable to this type of development than conditions in tribal societies with intense family ties, which have experienced and are still experiencing tremendous difficulties in establishing state structures.[11]

These factors were coupled with the influence of a very highly developed legal culture based on the tradition of Roman law and thus characterized by the separation of public and private institutions and hence by a clear distinction between civil society, organized on the basis of contract, and political society, governed by considerations of public interest.

The Roman legal system, later adapted by a number of European nations, is noteworthy for its ability to conceive and justify the existence of an autonomous state capable of defining the criteria of its own legitimacy. It should therefore come as no surprise that European countries subject to a strong Roman influence, like France, were prone to establish particularly strong states, whereas other countries like England, where the legal system was based largely on observation of the traditional practices prevalent in civil society and much less attention was paid to the definition of a separate public sphere, tended to construct much more limited states. Nor should it come as a surprise that the state did not emerge until after the rediscovery of the Justinian Code at the end of the eleventh century, at almost the same time as the first legal commentaries were being compiled in the thirteenth century. Finally, it is easy to understand why the process of political change encouraged the training of competent specialists in the law. The "legists" in the entourage of Philip the Fair were already, as we learn from Guénée, the heirs of a long tradition, which in France dates back to the mid-thirteenth century, well before the beginning of comparable traditions in Germany and Flanders. To put it another way, the rise of the state brought to prominence a group of men, distant ancestors of the modern civil servant, whose mastery of a specific body of knowledge put them in a position to wield greater power than their position in civil society by itself would have allowed; this in turn increased the differentiation of the political from the social system.[12]

This increased differentiation is particularly significant in that it was the result of simultaneous initiatives by the political system on the one hand and civil society on the other. For the political system the important change was the development of public law governing the sovereignty of the state. For civil society, the rediscovery of private law of contract and property was useful for staking out a private sphere independent of the prince's authority. Anderson shows how the development of the Western nation-state paralleled the development of property rights. Indeed, he shows that with respect to legal changes Europe's emergence from feudalism was unique, not at all comparable to the history of, say, Japan, where a system similar to the feudal system did develop but did not transform itself into a legal state as in Europe.[13]

The steady growth of an autonomous economy furnishes one last example of the European tendency to differentiate a public from a private domain. It is of course possible to look at this development as the result of changes in the economic infrastructure, which slowly spread throughout Europe. But the inadequacy of this way of viewing the situation is pointed up by the work of Louis Dumont and Karl Polanyi. The emergence of an autonomous economic sector is also affected by the cultural context, and it is not beyond the realm of possibility that changes in the social structure made necessary by this development were among the crucial factors in the formation of the Western nation-state.[14]

European culture was in fact strongly influenced by the Christian predilection for describing man as a responsible moral being, which leads to a description of society quite close to the one found in actor-centered sociological theories. Such a culture has an inherent tendency to foster individualized social relations.[15] Doubtless this belief in man's moral responsibility is responsible for the fact that Western culture tends to regard the economic sphere—and the relation of man to things--as embracing a coherent set of actions subject to laws of their own and perhaps even superior to other forms of action. Hence Western culture is to be distinguished from other cultures in which the economic sphere is thought of as embedded in, if not completely indistinguishable from, the surrounding social system.[16] Thus the principle of a separation of economy and society—a principle shared by both Karl Marx and Adam Smith—may be seen as a cultural matrix responsible in part for the shape of social change in Europe. Accordingly, the general principle of separation can be used to explain why the major crises in European history have been resolved (or at least responded to) by the formation of autonomous sectors, whether religious, political, or economic. The extensive development of the state in some European countries would, if this hypothesis is correct, be a result of the need to resort to separation of this sort on a large scale in order to resolve crises caused by exceptional resistance to change in traditional social formations.

The argument developed above is opposed to the functionalist account in two ways: first, in the contention that the differentiation of the political system and its development into a state are not features of social change in general but rather of social change in particular cultural contexts; and second, in the belief that changes of this sort are not determined by evolutionary necessity or some principle of social harmony but rather emerge as solutions to crises of reproduction or adaptation which develop in certain historically-specific social formations and which are largely independent of changes in the economic structure of those social formations.

6   The Transfer of the Idea of the State from Europe to Its Colonies

[handwritten notes: Kazancigil (1986) Badie & Birnbaum "Diffusionist"]

Like any political concept or, for that matter, like any idea at all, the idea of the state has been influential outside the countries in which it was first conceived. Some functionalists have recently moved away from the classical evolutionary position, according to which social and political change is always the result of some kind of endogenous social mechanism. These writers have begun to argue that along with the rise of the state came an "intellectual mobilization," which carried the idea of the state far beyond the borders of countries grappling with the problems created by an overdeveloped feudal system, such as France, and give it currency throughout Europe.[1] England, for example, where the centralization of the political system was not a live issue, was affected in some measure by the revival of Roman law, the growth of universities, the increase in the number of men with legal training, and the rise of bureaucracy. This "demonstration effect" did not lead to the development of a state (in the narrow sense) in England, but traces of its influence may be seen in the history of the Tudor and, even more so, the Stuart reigns. Conversely, English ideas about representative government, as embodied in the parliament of barons and the Magna Carta and, later, in the Puritan espousal of free elections, also spread across the Channel to the Continent, where they influenced the European concepts of the nation and of parliamentary government. In fact, it is probably because "nation" and "state" were at first symbiotic notions that the term "nation-state" is so common today, particularly in English and American sociology, even though the sources of the two ideas were different: the state was a French reaction against feudalism inspired by Roman culture, whereas the nation was an idea based on contract that originated in England, where social integration was never a real problem and the cultural influence of Protestantism was strong.

The idea of the state also moved eastward, but the flow in this direction was not as steady. Prussia and Russia both adopted some aspects of the state model, even though they were less well adapted socially and culturally to accept Western influences and even though the historical situation in both countries had little in common with the situation in the West in the period when the state first came to prominence. Neither Prussia nor Russia had a feudal past comparable to that of France, and the development of centralized political systems in both countries came largely in response to exogenous factors that had little in common with the social processes set in motion by the declining political power of the landed aristocracy. While the idea of the state did have some influence on both countries, the graft of some elements of that idea onto native stock produced two quite different kinds of hybrid that grew in strikingly dissimilar ways.

The peculiarity of the Prussian case is less obvious than that of the Russian, if only because Prussia lies physically closer to Europe. Still, the Germanic tradition that held sway in Prussia was considerably different from the Roman legacy that influenced the development of the state in France. Feudalism was late to develop in Prussia and did not take the same form there as in the West. Conditional tenure was unknown in the Holy Roman Empire, where the alod was the most common form of tenure and land was shared between a free peasantry and an aristocracy that depended in one degree or another on the emperor but did not develop a system of vassalage to any significant extent.[2] In fact, it was not until the twelfth century that the power of the emperor declined sufficiently to allow the local nobility to set itself up as a quasi-feudal aristocracy, which expelled free peasants from their land and claimed certain sovereign powers in the political and judicial realm. Thus the pattern of social change was the exact opposite of the French pattern: feudalism developed late and to a limited extent owing to the collapse of central political structures. After several centuries this process culminated in refeudalization and the subjugation of the peasantry, affording virtual autonomy to the all-powerful landowners.[3] Thus the direction of development east of the Elbe was *away* from the state. This was facilitated by the absence of conflicts within the aristocracy similar to those stemming from the complex web of relations between lord and vassal characteristic of Western feudalism. Furthermore, the progress of the monetary economy was slow in the East, and Eastern landlords did not have a powerful monarchy to contend with, since the Holy Roman Empire was slowly disintegrating.

When a centralized monarchy did emerge in Prussia in the eighteenth century, it was less the result of internal developments than a response to external threats, chiefly military pressures from the new states in the

West.[4] The influence of Western notions of the state explains the increasing centralization that took place in Prussia under Frederick William I and Frederick the Great. It also accounts for growing Prussian militarism, which was quick to develop. The graft of Western structures onto native stock did give rise in Prussia, though not in Russia, to a political system of a type similar to those found in the West. The Prussian state quickly assumed the role of defender of the nobility and of serfdom and defined itself in terms of the distinction between civil society and the state, a distinction characteristic of the type of state that emerged from the crisis of feudalism in the West. During the early eighteenth century the only way for the local administration to stake out an autonomous domain in Prussia was to come to an agreement with the lord of the locality in regard to the sharing of power. Thus the royal bureaucracy constantly had to compromise with civil society, which not only maintained its identity but continued to organize around certain old and powerful representative institutions.[5] The development of the Prussian state was marked by many of the same features and phases we have noted in other contexts: differentiation of a public from a private domain; the rise of a bureaucracy determined to win autonomy for itself and to escape the control of both the prince and particularistic interests; and a subtle mixture of intervention in the economy and respect for the laws of the market (something the tsars never learned how to achieve).

By contrast, the development of a centralized political system in Russia represents a far more radical departure from the familiar pattern of state building described in earlier chapters. In many respects the Russian case resembles the process of empire building more than that of state building. During the fourteenth century, Moscow rose to prominence and became the seed around which Russian society crystallized. With each new victory of the Russian princes over the Mongols, Moscow extended its control over an ever widening periphery. During the fifteenth and sixteenth centuries the central government was consolidated as the tsars fought to contain both the Tatars to the east and the newly powerful states of Europe to the west and worked to create an autonomous and indeed an autarchic political system. The Russian effort was directed first at conquering territory in the east and second at establishing an economy capable of meeting competition from the west.[6]

Thus political centralization in Russia came more in response to exogenous factors than to endogenous ones and had more to do with diplomatic and military considerations than with internal changes in the Russian social formation. Furthermore, it was the result more of decisions taken by the prince alone than of demands stemming from new economic elites. Nevertheless, the end result of the centralization process was the emergence of a number of institutions strongly influenced by Western ideas of the state. Thus Ivan III instinctively turned responsibility for newly conquered provinces over to a governor *(namestnik)* authorized to set up a local bureaucracy. At the same time a central bureaucracy *(prikaz)* grew up in Moscow, staffed by specialized personnel *(diaki)* and governed by a rudimentary administrative code *(Soudebnik)*. Ivan IV merely finished the job by creating the *Oprichnina,* which gave the Tsar a monopoly of police and military powers at the expense of the boyars.[7]

Here the resemblance between Russia and the West ends, however. Russian centralization was based on different assumptions and responded to different needs, and the resulting political system was bound to be different from the Western type of state in a number of respects. For one thing, civil society was almost entirely absorbed by the expanding Russian state. In order to meet its own needs the tsarist system directly appropriated the conquered lands in Siberia and established a system of land tenure that enabled it to make temporary grants of land to its soldiers, without giving them the land *(pomestie)* outright. In addition, the prestige and status of the Russian aristocracy, both old and new, were subject to the pleasure of the prince and to his willingness to allow the nobility access to political life. In other words, the tsarist system revived a model of government in which the social and political systems were completely identified. This identification was facilitated by the fact that the Russian Orthodox religion had always rejected any form of separation of powers. The Russian Church gave its blessings to Ivan III when he proclaimed himself tsar, thereby legitimating his rule.

It is characteristic of the state of affairs in Russia, moreover, that whenever the tsarist regime did attempt to adopt certain features of Western states, the result was only to encourage still closer identification of society and polity. Peter I, for example, attempted to professonalize the bureaucracy by separating the civil service from the military, requiring a period of apprenticeship for all functionaries, and establishing fixed criteria for promotion.[8] Peter III extended this policy by ending compulsory service for the aristocracy and setting a limit to the number of civil servants. On the whole, however, these measures only made the aristocracy even more dependent on the tsar and thus made the social system even more dependent on the political system. During the nineteenth century there were constant efforts to prevent the growth of

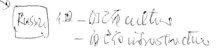

autonomous groups within civil society, such as associations, interest
groups, and even industrial enterprises not controlled by the state. Steps
were also taken to prevent the creation of autonomous local governments
or even representative bodies, at both the local and the national level.
Thus, even though Russia was clearly exposed to the influence of
Western ideas of the state, it evolved a form of political organization
quite unlike any found in the West. Russian culture and Russian social
infrastructures were quite different from their Western counterparts.
But there are other countries even more different from the West than
Russia was. When Western political ideas are imported into such countries, the result is generally the emergence of hybrid forms of government, which are often antipathetic to the character of the societies in
which they develop and able to endure only by resorting to violence
or totalitarian rule.

This has indeed been the case in many third-world societies. Admit-
tedly, any approach that looks at these societies as constituting a homo-
genous category is liable to all the criticisms we have already leveled at
modernization theory. But such an approach does seem justified in one
respect. European culture and therefore the basic ideas behind the rise
of the state are alien to the countries of the third world. These countries must participate in an economic system that is largely beyond
their control. Most of them have suffered military conquest and colonial
rule. Hence state building in these societies has largely been a matter of
imitating models developed elsewhere, in industrial societies of either
East or West, and artificially superimposed, with or without local con-
sent, on economic, social, and political structures shaped by other ways
of thinking.

The introduction of Western ideas of the state has been associated
with circumstances that vary widely from one country to the next, however. Countries adjacent to Europe encountered Western political ideas
in the context of a more general influence of European culture, encouraged in part by respect for European military and economic exploits. In
the early eighteenth century, when European nations were for the first
time placing the Turks on the defensive both militarily and economically,
the Ottoman sultan Ahmad III and the sadr-e-azam Ibrahim Pasha inaugurated the "Age of Tulips" with careful study of European laws and
forms of government. The so-called *tanzimat* reforms begun a century
later gave official recognition of sorts to the European idea of the state
and gave it currency throughout the Ottoman Empire by setting up a
partly secular bureaucracy divided into a number of ministries not sub-

ject to the authority of the sheik-al-Islam. Other reforms included the institution of a secular legal system covering such aspects of social life as trade and the penal system and the establishment of a number of specialized technical schools, foremost among which was a military academy established in 1834 and modeled on similar institutions in Europe.[9] Western ideas were also influential in Persia from the Safavid era on. They achieved institutional status in the mid-nineteenth century under Nasered-din Shah and Amir Kabir. Once again Western ideas were first adopted in governmental reforms and later influenced the army and educational system.[10]

In contrast to this pattern of Western influence was the role of Western political ideas in countries colonized by the nations of Europe. In these countries the introduction of Western "political technology" was not only more sudden and systematic but also less far-reaching in its effects. Experience with colonial administrations did undoubtedly pave the way for state building after independence. Similarities between African and European political systems that are still apparent today can be explained by cultural influences transmitted through colonial administrations. But the bureaucracies set up by the colonial powers were designed mainly for the purpose of colonial rule and did not permit the development of centralized political systems capable of controlling highly segmented peripheries where traditional modes of government remained potent.[11] Not only was the graft of Western structures onto native stock artificial; but even these peculiar hybrids were prevented from developing naturally by the fact that the colonial powers generally impeded progress in the division of labor within colonial societies, and thus prevented civil society from adjusting to its imported political structures. The colonial powers were also at pains to limit the growth of native administrative and economic elites, as in Algeria. The end result was only to make the hybrid plants that did take root seem even more outlandish and unsuited to their surroundings.[12]

Beyond the diffusion of Western cultural influence, we must also take account of the consequences of the political order prevailing in the world. Through international law and other codified value systems, the existing world order promotes the idea that the state is the one valid model of political development and that any country that wishes to win the respect of its neighbors and achieve developed status must work to construct a true modern state.[13]

No matter how much local elites may have internalized Western political ideas, the truth is that the Western model has only been transplanted in an abstract and formal sense and has not really worked in third-world societies. It is a model that has been introduced artificially, sometimes by force, sometimes voluntarily when traditional forms of government have been rejected because of unfair accusations that they were responsible for economic and military failures. To this day the "state" is no more than an imported artifact in both Africa and Asia, a pale copy of utterly alien European social and political systems, a foreign body that is not only inefficient and a burden on society but also a fomenter of violence.

Signs of failure are encountered first at the structural level. States in the third world are usually no more than fragmented bureaucracies. Unlike their European counterparts, the various departments of these bureaucracies are not integrated into the political community and not counterbalanced by an autonomous civil society with a structure of its own. Countries in the third world have weak institutional foundations, so that their rulers lack independent sources of power and legitimacy and therefore cannot stand up to their bureaucracies or use them as instruments of consistent and rational policy.[14] At the same time the low level of economic development and social mobilization means that civil society is not sufficiently organized to benefit in any real sense from bureaucratic regulation and coordination. The fact is that in most third-world countries the bureaucracy has no control over the economy, which is largely dependent on foreign investment, so that bureaucracy's functions are limited to routine matters of policy and administration.

Thus the function of the bureaucracy has been distorted, and this is one more reason for the failure of the Western graft to "take" in third-world countries. Isolated from the rest of society, these third-world bureaucracies are mainly engaged in supporting and reproducing a political class which often governs what is in effect a mere marginal sector of the local economy. This ruling class takes its power from many sources[15] and, largely by way of corruption, confiscates much of the available wealth.[16] The persistence of clientele relations also helps to explain how bureaucracies of a personal and patrimonial type have been able to endure in these countries, even though their only purpose is to aggrandize an all-powerful ruling elite.[17]

The situation is made even worse by the existence of a vicious circle. Bureaucracy and other Western political ideas were incompatible with local tradition in many third-world countries. As a result, political development has split third-world societies in two: one segment of society derives its legitimacy from the desire for modernization, while the other strives to preserve national traditions without any effort of adaptation or reform. Such a split was evident in Egypt under the khedive Ismael in the eighteenth-century Ottoman Empire,[18] as well as in the political system of Turkey under Kemal, which was able to function only by excluding the peasantry from the modernization process.[19] The more the "state" tries to develop itself, the more its claims to monopoly meet with opposition, forcing it to cut itself off from the rest of society. The more the state fails to exert control over the rest of society, the more it is forced to increase the pressure and push for even greater mobilization. This leads to reliance on totalitarian methods, which are fundamentally inimical to the principles of differentiation and autonomy essential to the state's identity.[20]

It is wrong, however, to think that the failure of Western political ideas in the third world is due only to economic backwardness and that further development would insure their success. The real reasons for the failure lie elsewhere. One is somewhat paradoxical: the economic dominance of the West has undermined its cultural hegemony. The states of Africa, Asia, and South America are currently forced to confront a Western monopoly of much of the world's wealth; and their economic, financial, and technological dependence only serves to reproduce this state of affairs.[21] This situation threatens to get even worse, owing to the steady growth of multinational firms, which may replace the nation-state as the fundamental unit of the international community.[22]

An even more important reason for the failure of Western political ideas is that the increasing importance of the state in third-world countries is based on two fundamental misconceptions, which the end of foreign domination has done nothing to eliminate. To begin with, the economic, social, and political problems faced by third-world countries are utterly unlike the problems faced by European countries when states first emerged in Europe. Europe had to deal with a crisis of feudalism involving the private ownership of land by feudal lords. Most third-world societies, particularly in Africa, are currently faced with a quite different sort of crisis, involving the persistence of tribal structures, the crucial importance of kinship, and the limited individualization of property rights in land.[23] Whereas European societies had to find ways to integrate already existing economic elites, the developing countries today need to create a market economy, to say nothing of a full-blown industrial society, from the ground up. Finally, whereas Renaissance Europe had only to contend with a gradual increase in the demand for popular participation, an increase more or less kept in check by organized civil society, today's newly independent societies have to face a much more dramatic rise in the desire for participation, which traditional allegiances by themselves cannot hold back.

Such different issues require different solutions. In these circumstances it is hard to see how a state based on Roman law can really survive in the third world, when in fact it was never really able even to cross the English Channel from the Continent.

This brings us to the second misconception mentioned above. As the product of a culture based largely on the principle of differentiation, the state has not been able to achieve institutional form in societies dominated by "organic religions" such as Islam or Hinduism, which reject the idea of a temporal or secular domain distinct from the spiritual.[24] What is true of religion also holds good for the other components of a culture. Hence it seems clear that the state born in Renaissance Europe and today held forth as a model for states everywhere is not suited to the kinds of cultures that have shaped most third-world societies.

It is naive to think that economic modernization will dispose of this kind of objection. But it is equally illusory to assume that the persistence of cultural variety rules out any kind of innovation. A number of orientalists have shown that the same function performed by secularization in Europe can be accomplished in other ways in Islamic societies. In particular, change can occur if the link between traditional authority and sacred authority is broken and if modern, profane values are allowed to influence existing religious values but without relegating them to a distinct spiritual domain. Bear in mind that resistance to change in the Middle East has not been due to the place of religion in Middle Eastern societies but rather to the way religion has been used ever since the time of the Ommiad caliphate, namely, to enable the ruling class to hold on to power and to preserve the existing social structure.[25] It was precisely in reaction to this use of religion that Afqāni developed his Islamic reform movement and Mohammed Abduh organized an opposition movement in Egypt at the end of the nineteenth century.[26] Innovation may well be encouraged by many aspects of Islamic culture: for example, consensus is a central theme recognized as a source of law by the classical schools of Islamic law, and this might be used as a basis for organizing popular participation in politics and establishing new forms of legitimation.[27]

Part Three

State, Center, and Power
in Contemporary Societies

What we hope to have shown thus far is that the state developed within a historical process that was unique to certain Western societies. Even in the West, however, civil society has at times been able to make do without a state. It has often been able to organize itself and by doing so to prevent the development of a state with some claim to the right to wield absolute power. Wherever a state exists, the entire social system is affected. Civil society invariably organizes around the state once the state has come into existence. The nature of the political system has a significant impact on class relations, that is, on the interaction between the nobility, the bourgeoisie, the working class, and, more recently, the "middle classes." Class relations vary widely depending on whether there is a highly institutionalized state or a mere political center whose main function is to coordinate the activities of civil society. It is still possible even today to distinguish between political systems in which there is both a center and a state (France), a state but no center (Italy), a center but no true state (Great Britain and the United States), and neither a center nor a true state (Switzerland).[1] In the first two cases the state dominates civil society and is responsible for its organization, albeit in different degrees. In the last two cases civil society organizes itself. It is therefore possible to distinguish between societies in which the state attempts to run the social system through a powerful bureaucracy (of which France is the ideal type, with Prussia, Spain, and Italy exhibiting similar trajectories) and societies in which there is no need for a strong state and governing bureaucracy because civil society is capable of organizing itself (of which Great Britain is the ideal type, with the United States and "consociational democracies" [see below] such as Switzerland exhibiting similar trajectories). While we cannot here methodically trace the history of all these various states and political centers,[2] we hope to show that the relations among the various components of the ruling class in different social systems are determined in some cases by the formation of the state, in others by the mere constitution of a political center.

7   Government via the State: Power to the Bureaucracy

The State Model: France

The state whose construction has occupied all of French history may be taken as the ideal type of *the* state. Prussia, Spain, and Italy all followed similar historical trajectories. In no other case, however, was the process of differentiation and institutionalization carried as far as in France. In a sense, once the French state had succeeded in achieving a position of absolute rule, it acquired the capacity to hold on to its sovereign power. From Hugh Capet to Louis XIV, from the French Revolution to Napoleon III and the Gaullist regime, the French state has steadily expanded its control over civil society and constituted itself as an autonomous power, an immense and hermetic administrative machine capable of dominating all peripheral power centers. If the state is defined as a system of permanently institutionalized roles which has the exclusive right to the legitimate use of force, whereby it exerts sovereign power over a given territory, including its most remote provinces, and defends the borders of that territory against foreign incursion, and if that system is institutionalized in the form of a political and administrative machine run by civil servants recruited on an impersonal basis according to meritocratic criteria, then the French state must be seen as the ideal type of *the* state. That it should have become so was in no sense foreordained. The assertion that the French Republic is "one and indivisible," contained in the 1793 constitution, does no more than record the success of an effort to achieve political centralization that in its beginnings was nothing if not risky in the extreme. For a long time the center commanded the loyalty of almost no one, and yet it was the center that was called upon to embody the state. Not until the Renaissance do we witness the birth of the absolutist model of the state, and not until the eighteenth century do we find Frenchmen beginning to think of France's borders as "natural," as later became commonplace. It was at around the same time that loyalty to the nation-state began to be seen as a universal imperative, taking precedence over conflicting loyalties to religious, social, cultural, and linguistic groups. During the feudal period the power of the "center" was still very weak: Hugh Capet reigned over the Ile-de-France but not over Anjou, Aquitaine, or Normandy. Feudal lords administered justice, raised taxes, and barricaded themselves in castles with their own personal armies. Cities won the right to govern themselves, and "feudal anarchy" led to complete fragmentation of authority.[1]

The absolutist state formed slowly as royal power was consolidated and began to whittle away at the independence of the lords and the autonomy of the towns. Through alliances and conquests the various subsystems within the society were linked to the center. Those who had chosen to ally themselves with foreign powers in order to strengthen their hand against the central government, such as the dukes of Burgundy, who fought on the side of the English during the Hundred Years' War, were forced to declare their allegiance to the kind of France.[2] It was in France that the first standing army was established, an army fed, clothed, and paid by the royal government.[3] By the end of the Middle Ages a limited form of absolutism had been established: the center slowly transformed itself into an absolutist state and consolidated its authority. Toward that end it established an administration whose power was destined to grow steadily, thereby contributing by degrees to the institutionalization of the state. The king encouraged the growth of a central bureaucracy and of a series of councils in which state policy was elaborated. At the same time, he worked to break the resistance of the feudal lords by strengthening the regional administration, headed by the *baillis* and *sénéchaux*. This regional administration steadily chipped away at the jurisdiction of the traditional authorities. In contrast to what took place in England, however, the French local administration was quick to become institutionalized: royal officeholders soon obtained guarantees of immunity from removal from their posts and set up local bureaucracies, initially in the form of *bailliage* councils. These testified so eloquently to the institutionalization of the state that it has been possible to say that they "protected the kingship from the king"; behind the logic of absolutism, these councils presaged another logic, that of the nascent state, distinct not only from civil society but also from the person of the prince.[4]

Furthermore, in 1551 the royal officials known as *maîtres des requêtes* were named *"commissaires* for the execution of the king's orders," whereby they were distinguished from other officials who owned their offices. The practice of selling royal offices nevertheless continued to spread. In 1604 the so-called Paulette gave officeholders the right to pass their offices on to designated heirs. The owners of offices undoubtedly acquired the capacity to act independently of the great nobles, but the danger was that they might also attempt to thwart the will of the king. The *commissaire,* as distinct from the *officier,* did not own his office and presumably had no ties to local forces bent on resisting the central government. As an instrument of the state, the *commissaire* "was not an officeholder but a functionary."[5] The position of *commissaire* later gave rise to the *intendants* and the *préfets,* officials who helped to transform the central government into a state.

It was not until the seventeenth and eighteenth centuries, however, that the power of the absolute monarchy ceased to be limited by various contracts, customs, and privileges. In keeping with a variety of pragmatic, theocratic, and rational concerns, absolutism established the sovereignty of the state over the nation. Such theorists of absolutism as the abbé Fleury, Domat, and Loyseau justified the state's paramount position and followed in the footsteps of the Renaissance legists in rediscovering the *jus publicum,* or public law, which had come into being at the end of the Roman era only to disappear into oblivion during the reign of the Merovingians and Carolingians and throughout the feudal period.[6] The new distinction that was drawn between the *jus publicum* and the *jus privatum* testifies by itself to the newfound autonomy of the state, to the gradual differentiation of the state from civil society, and to the birth of a public space. The modernization of the legal system and the use by the state of legal theorists contributed significantly to the centralization of power in the hands of the king. Up to the nineteenth century the autonomy of the system of administrative law steadily increased. The institution of private property was also reinforced, thereby encouraging, in one way or another, the growth of a market.

With absolutism came the growth of institutions in which it was possible to divine the shape of the future French state. The old provincial administrations were dismantled in order to destroy local allegiances. They were replaced by administrative units known as *généralités,* forerunners of the *départements.* Each *généralité* was ruled by an *intendant,* an official with direct access to the central executive and presumably immune from the influence of local patrons (just as the modern-day prefect establishes a direct line of communication from the *département* to the central government in Paris and makes decisions that are presumed to be unbiased by entangling local alliances). What is more, the *intendants* were able to enlist the services of assistants *(sous-intendants* or *subdélégués),* with administrative personnel at all ranks being recruited either among commoners, among the nobility of other regions, or from the king's entourage.[7] The autonomy of the towns was smashed. Richelieu systematically destroyed castles all over France in order to eliminate the last vestiges of independence. In 1726 a standing army was created for the same reason, establishing a monopoly over the use of force and doing away with personal armies under the command of various peripheral authorities.[8] Starting with Le Tellier and Louvois, military organization was placed under the control of army intendants dispatched by the central government, who enjoyed full powers of command. In order to prevent rebellions of the sort attempted by Condé in the mid-seventeenth century, the state "nationalized" all army regiments and assumed responsibility for clothing and paying the troops.

By degrees the absolutist state assumed responsibility for international relations and consolidated its strength by accentuating its military vocation.[9] A professional army dominated by mercenaries and controlled by civilian *intendants* appointed by the king and generally chosen outside the great aristocratic families gave the state a redoubtable power and consequently a considerable degree of autonomy in its actions.[10] To carry its military policies through successfully (and to maintain an army that numbered more than 300,000 men under Louis XIV), the monarchy was forced to strengthen its system of tax collection. The French government collected four times as much in taxes as the English government in the early seventeenth century.[11] New taxes applicable to all royal subjects, such as the *capitation,* were instituted, and the fiscal administration was either refurbished or turned over to private financiers, the so-called farmers general, who collected taxes under the watchful eye of the *intendants.*[12] The regulation of the economic life of the nation became despotic: every aspect of the operation of the economy was determined by state policy. First under Richelieu and then under Colbert, the state set up manufacturing enterprises, offered subsidies and privileges as a way of orienting production, and regulated both foreign and internal trade. The "triumph of *étatisme*"[13] implicit in this mercantilist economic policy was such that one author has said that "from 1683 to the inauguration of the first five-year plan by the Soviet government in Russia, no conscious and directed effort to develop a nation's industrial life was so prolonged, so thorough, so permeating, so far-reaching as that of Colbert."[14]

In order to carry out these interventionist policies and control their consequences, a powerful police force was instituted (the *maréchaussée*).

The press was controlled, and the government even began publishing a state newspaper, the *Gazette de France,* in 1761. Another indication of state control over social life may be seen in the Gallican Church, which influenced individual consciences, as well as in the supervision of French universities and education.[15] With the progressive installation of the various components of the administrative machine, the autonomy of the state increased by degrees. It is in this sense that we may say that "absolutism is above all the perfected form of bureaucratic organization."[16]

Thanks to this growing institutionalization, the state gained both independence and durability. It appeared to have its own characteristic identity, to the point that the king came increasingly to be seen as nothing more than the first servant of the state. Hence it was not so much the king as the state itself that wielded absolute power. Both civilian and military bureaucracies grew steadily, and the locus of political activity came to reside more and more in the various councils that controlled the different departments of the bureaucracy.[17] As Tocqueville has pointed out, "under the *ancien régime* as in our own day, not a single city, town, or village, not even the smallest hamlet, not a single hospital, workhouse, convent or college could exercise the least independence with regard to its own affairs or administer its own property as it saw fit. Then as now the administration controlled the lives of all Frenchmen."[18] Even if there are obvious exaggerations in this interpretation, since the peripheries, the dominated social classes, and the towns all managed to put up some sort of resistance against the encroachments of the state, and the state itself was infiltrated by representatives of the dominant social classes and groups, so that its independence and institutional autonomy were limited, still Tocqueville's account is an accurate description of an ideal type, a model in which the state and its administration rule over every aspect of life in civil society. The state Tocqueville has in mind is the one that continued its assaults on civil society during the French Revolution and the Empire, thereby moving toward greater autonomy of action. As Tocqueville goes on to say, "This was a government the likes of which had not been seen since the fall of the Roman Empire. The Revolution created this new power, or, rather, this new power rose from the ruins that the Revolution left in its wake."[19]

In order to keep a closer watch over civil society and destroy local allegiances once and for all so as to impose a uniform system of rules elaborated by the central government, the Constituent Assembly divided the territory of France into eighty-three *départements,* an action that disrupted the structure of existing regional communities. Like the *gén-*

éralités of the ancien régime, the *départements* made it easier for the state to exert control over civil society. To head the *départements,* prefects were appointed for the first time in 1800, replacing the old royal *intendants.* Like the *commissaires* of old, the prefects answered only to the central government. They had complete control over all aspects of life in their *départements* and eliminated the last vestiges of local autonomy — at a slightly later date they even acquired the power to appoint game wardens in the most remote villages. The new hierarchy of central government, prefect, and subprefect replaced the old hierarchy of king, *intendant,* and *subdélégué* associated with the absolute monarchy. From this point on, a system of highly centralized bureaucracies extended its influence over the entire nation. A police official responsible to the central government was assigned to each town of over five thousand inhabitants, and the *gendarmerie nationale* assumed responsibility for maintaining law and order throughout France.[20] Thus, as the eighteenth century began, the state was able to tighten its grip on civil society. Beginning in 1798, conscription served to guarantee the unity of the nation, embodied in the state, against the foreign enemies massing on France's borders. Within France, citizens identified more and more with their state, all other loyalties apparently having evaporated.

Insofar as the state stood for the sovereignty of the nation, its legitimacy was enhanced and it was consequently able to claim greater autonomy of action. The public domain was governed by a body of administrative law already rediscovered by the monarchy: the administration was not required to abide by the ordinary system of law, since its operation came under the jurisdiction of the Conseil d'Etat (An VIII). The state ceased to be a part of civil society, or so it seemed, since it now enjoyed prerogatives that enabled it to carry out its mission by resorting to various forms of administrative procedure: in this sense it has been said that "administrative law is the common law of the public authorities."[21]

The process of autonomization may also be seen at work in the growing separation of Church and state, the gap between the two widening steadily from the time of the French Revolution to the final break, which came in 1903-5 with the passage of a series of laws redefining the status of the Church, a milestone marking the state's achievement of legitimacy in its own right. Secularism may thus be seen as one of the primary indicators of the progress of state building in France, marking the step-by-step separation of the state from all other social systems. Since we are here regarding France as the ideal type of a state political system, it should come as no surprise that the French pushed secularism to its extreme limit. Conversely, from the time of the Revolution on, the state increasingly arrogated to itself the right to dispense the light of wisdom, more or less completely stripping the Church of this privilege. Just as the monarchy had concerned itself with education as a way of shoring up its own legitimacy, so too did the state gradually tighten its control of university and secondary education, determining who was appointed to teaching positions, how much they were paid, and what and how they taught. The teachers in turn did their utmost to bestow legitimacy upon the state, whose role was said to be impartial, functional, and rational. This was especially true of the teachers of the Third Republic.

Space does permit a detailed account of how the French state achieved full differentiation. The absolutist, revolutionary, and Napoleonic periods were all crucial, but it is important to point out that the bureaucracy continued to grow even during the years when liberalism reigned supreme. The nineteenth century may have been the golden age of liberal capitalism, but, unlike England, France then had an "economic administration that was not merely Napoleonic but downright *louis-quatorzienne.*"[22] Contrary to conventional wisdom on the subject, the steady increase of centralization was never disrupted from the Ancien Régime to the nineteenth century and on down to the present. The state became more and more institutionalized as the power of the administration increased. Important milestones along the way were the regime of Napoleon III, the two world wars and their immediate aftermath, and finally the Gaullist period.

During the nineteenth century, Tocqueville and later Taine and Leroy-Beaulieu focused attention on the constantly growing power of the state administration. As Leroy-Beaulieu stressed, however, "the state is not society's brain; it has no qualification, no aptitude, no mission to lead society or to blaze its trails."[23] In the same period other writers declared themselves to be in favor of centralization and saluted it as "a pure form of Gallicanism."[24] The fact is that centralization has been chronically on the rise ever since the nineteenth century. From the Second Empire to the Gaullist regime we find the same Colbertian strategy of intervention and control with regard to the economy. Influenced by Saint-Simonianism, the administration of the Second Empire stimulated industry, built railroads, and shook up the bourgeoisie. At a later date Gaullism, with its faith in the mysteries of planning, took similar initiatives in order to transform the French economy. The state has been in the habit of imposing its policy on civil society. The economic plan worked out by the administration is supposed to become the *grande affaire* of France. As in the time of the absolute monarchy, the state has not hesitated to create its own industries. From the period between the First and Second World Wars until today, there has been steady growth in the number of bureaucractic departments and a concomitant increase in the number of state-owned industries, public agencies to assist industrial firms, semi-public corporations, and so forth. The welfare state is embodied in the social security administration and other activist government agencies.

The state has, in every respect, apparently tightened its grip on civil society. To that end it has used the various corps of civil servants trained in special schools, the first of which were established during the first half of the nineteenth century. More recently, the Ecole Nationale d'Adminis-tration (ENA), founded in 1945, has risen to a position of great promi-nence, but it merely continues a long-standing tradition of elite adminis-trative institutions. French civil servants are recruited on the basis of competitive examinations and meritocratic criteria and are seen increas-ingly, as the phrase goes, as mere "functions in action." Civil servants are bound by law to make no public statements about their work, and in the upper reaches of the administration, where the ideology of the general interest reigns supreme, it is common for officials to regard themselves as agents of the state. Accordingly, a system of specialized roles has grown up, and the administration has thereby developed into a highly institutionalized and autonomous organization. The *grands corps* serve increasingly as the cutting edge of state action, with mem-bers staffing posts in the military, nationalized industry, and the public service sector, as well as in agencies concerned with regional planning and economic development. Highly professional and well grounded in economics, these senior civil servants enhance the capacity of the state to act independently.[25]

The state that history has constructed in France, viewed as an ideal type, has thus successfully carried through the process of institutionali-zation. Under the absolute monarchy, the bureaucracy had not yet totally differentiated itself from civil society. Since some *intendants* were recruited from the nobility and the *grande bourgeoisie,* for example, it is hard to be sure just what degree of autonomy they may actually have enjoyed. For Tocqueville, "the administrative functionaries, vir-tually all *bourgeois,* already formed a specific class with its own peculiar outlook, traditions, virtues, honor, and pride. This class was the aristoc-racy of the new society, fully formed and vital even before the Revolu-tion, which it awaited solely to clear its way."[26] François Furet is right, however, in pointing out that this analysis is quite "inaccurate,"[27] in that the funtionaries in question were hardly all *bourgeois* and, what is more, subscribed to different political values. Accordingly, even if the state was able at this time to count on the services of men it appointed itself, it was not yet fully institutionalized and the administration was a long way from being "in power": it was not, according to Furet, sufficiently institutionalized to give rise to a system of specific roles. Still, Denis Richet has managed, though with many hesitations, to show that senior civil servants formed a "unified corps, despite the variety in their family backgrounds."[28] For Richet, the "king's men" may have come from the same families as the *noblesse de robe,* but they nevertheless "distinguished themselves [from their relatives] by their rigorous, authoritarian, and sometimes leveling notion of state service."[29]

While all historians are agreed that centralization under the Ancien Régime was considerable, some argue that the centralization process gave rise to an institution sufficiently differentiated to serve as the foundation of an authentic state, whereas others contend that centralization served the interests mainly of the bourgeoisie and aristocracy, as it was from these two classes that the administration drew its staff. The same ambiguity remains when we look at the nineteenth and twentieth centuries. If we confine our attention to two special cases, the period of the Second Empire and the recent Gaullist regime, we find in both a high degree of institutionalization, comparable to that of the absolute monarchy. During the Second Empire the state machinery was considerably reinforced, centralization was accentuated, and the prefects extended their control over their *départements.* The autonomy of the administration increased. Senior civil servants were required to pass examinations; many were the sons of other senior civil servants and spent long years in the service of the state. Like the *intendants* under Louis XIV, however, they were drawn from the well-off classes of society. Still, they tended even more than the *intendants* to become bureaucrats or functionaries in the modern sense of the term, acquiring specific skills and thereby strengthening the system of interdependent roles constituting the government bureaucracy.[30] At the inception of the Fourth Republic a new comprehensive civil service statute, the establishment of the Ecole Nationale d'Administration, and the inauguration of economic planning set the stage for the most recent resurgence of a highly institutionalized state in France, the Gaullist Fifth Republic. Highly professionalized civil servants recruited on a meritocratic basis wielded even greater power than their counterparts under the monarchy or the Second

Empire. A veritable "republic of functionaries" came into being and extended its control to the periphery either through the prefects or through such specialized agencies as the *Délégation à l'aménagement du territoire et à l'action régionale* (DATAR), a sort of national planning commission. As during the period of the Revolution all of France fell under the sway of the central government. Guided in their actions by the ideology of the general interest, senior civil servants thought of themselves as the agents of an impartial, powerful, and functional state that stood at some remove from civil society. Though still recruited from privileged social strata, they saw themselves even more than before as "functions in action," that is, they acted, or so they believed, not in accordance with their class background or as dictated by their political beliefs but rather in keeping with the role they played in the governmental institution. Such behavior is essential to the operation of the institutionalized state. Quite plainly no state is ever fully autonomous, not even in France: there is always a variety of ties linking civil servants, whether Louis XIV's *intendants* or the Fifth Republic's prefects, to civil society. In particular, clientele relations grow up between state functionaries and various private interests on the periphery, and these tend to diminish the state's autonomy of action.[31] If we take a comparative point of view, however, the overwhelming impression is that no other country in the world has a government as highly institutionalized as the government of France.

This high degree of institutionalization leads to a novel set of relations among the various groups within the ruling class. To the extent that the state administration successfully achieves independence (as an organization) from the ruling class and civil society as a whole, it comes to be seen as the only truly representative organ, and the parliament is thereby deprived of its representative function. Since the state bureaucracy claims to represent the general interest as opposed to the special interests that make their voices heard in parliament, it assumes the right to intervene through its various agencies and to control social life in general. Thus under the Fifth Republic more than one-third of the ministers have been senior civil servants. These have generally been men who have made their careers in the state apparatus, as opposed to the typical member of parliament, who has strong local roots. From this point of view the high degree of institutionalization can be seen in the complete identification of the executive power with the high administration, which makes the state less susceptible to the influence of local clients and pressure groups. The state has also extended its control over the periphery by dispatching senior civil servants to stand for seats in parliament and to run for the position of mayor in various major cities. Similarly, it has strengthened its hold on the economy by appointing top civil servants to head public service corporations, nationalized banks, semipublic firms, and so on. It has also extended its control, it would appear, by sending some of its agents to work in major firms in the private sector, where they frequently occupy top management positions. Although this tentacular expansion of the state has at certain times receded (between the time of the July Monarchy, say, and that of the "republic of deputies," or, again, under Giscard, who greatly reduced the width of the gulf between the state and the ruling class),[32] it has never been seriously threatened. Perhaps the reason for this is that proponents of expansion have been able to describe it as the natural result of a long historical tendency toward centralization, which has succeeded in producing a state that is at last capable of setting itself the goal of "policing" the whole of society.

A Case of Incomplete Institutionalization: Prussia

Prussia followed a pattern of development similar to that of France, although for various reasons a fully institutionalized state never emerged there. The Holy Roman Empire had proved incapable of developing into a state itself and had thus been forced to allow princes and towns falling within its purview to increase their power and autonomy. Well after the Holy Roman Empire had for all practical purposes ceased to exist, the Hohenzollerns established their power over Prussian territory during the seventeenth century. Unlike the French monarchy, they were not forced to resort to violence to establish their authority over peripheral centers of power. Prussia controlled its borders from the outset and the government did not need to secure its frontiers at the same time it was working to achieve autonomy. On the other hand the state that developed in Prussia was more artificial than the one in France; it was an imported state.

In Prussia the state was founded on the military power of the Hohenzollerns and set in a harsh country inhabited by soldier-peasants and noble landlords, or Junkers. It was a police state *(Polizeistaat)* in which the power of the government was absolute. The army and the police played key roles in the "Sparta of the North," which was nothing less than a garrison state. The monarchy commanded the full obedience of an army of functionaries as well. The Prussian civil service of the late seventeenth and eighteenth century had no real autonomy and no protection under the law. The civil service was totally dominated by the army, infiltrated by the nobility, and ruled by the monarch. Hence the state had no autonomy. Prussian development differs from French development in that the nobility in Prussia always identified with the state: the Junkers were incorporated into the administration at the exact same time the French nobles were being pushed out. No true state could develop in Prussia because the monarchy was absolute and the influence of the Junker aristocracy was pervasive. Through the formidable bureaucratic apparatus the aristocracy controlled the entire country.[33] The aristocracy also controlled the administration at the local level: the central government's representatives in rural areas, the *Landräte* (counterparts of the French *intendants*), were chosen from a list drawn up by local nobles. Even though the *Landräte* were responsible to the central government, they acted as representatives of the landed aristocracy to a far greater extent than the *intendants* in France.[34]

Other factors also impeded the development of a true state. The army, which was led by the Junker aristocracy, actually controlled the civilian bureaucracy, whereas in France, under Louis XIV, royal agents supervised the military even on the field of battle. In a garrison state of this sort no real autonomy of action is possible. By the same token the attempt to develop a rational, impersonal bureaucracy was doomed to failure because every functionary owed the monarch unquestioning loyalty *(Treue)*. The Prussian *Staatsdiener* swore on oath of allegiance and loyalty to the king. He placed himself entirely at the king's service. This "loyalty" imparted an emotional character to public office that is hardly consistent with Weber's notion of bureaucracy. This emotional relationship to the monarch left a profound imprint on the minds of Prussian civil servants and colors the outlook of civil servants in Germany even today.

These various factors account for the peculiar pattern of Prussian development. But it is nonetheless important to take note of the various common features of both the French and the Prussian patterns, which distinguish them from the Anglo-Saxon model (notwithstanding the crucial difference with regard to the role played by the aristocracy). At a very early stage Prussia adopted a mercantile policy similar to the one adopted by France. Economic interventionism in Prussia took the form of the creation of royal manufactories together with the development of a tax system considerably more effective than the one developed in France: by the end of the seventeenth century Prussian tax collectors were taking three times as much from each citizen as French tax collectors. As in France, the Prussian government set up a system of technical schools intended to train personnel for the state, such as the *Bauakademie,* which is comparable with the French Ecole des Ponts et Chausées. Also inspired by French models were the military academies, which trained officers for the army. Here, too, France and Prussia were both radically different from Great Britain.[35]

These state instruments paved the way for the creation of a series of *Zollvereine* or customs unions in the nineteenth century, reflecting the importance of the state's role in creating a market. Within the borders of the new German Empire, the state played an important role, as in France, in the process of industrialization, where intervention by political and administrative elites was indispensable owing to the relative economic backwardness of the German nation.[36] As Barrington Moore has emphasized, Germany attempted to make a "revolution from above" and thereby "to modernize without changing [its] social structure. The only way out of this dilemma was militarism which united the upper classes."[37] Carried out under the leadership of the aristocracy, this mode of industrialization set limits to the expansion of the bourgeoisie and effectively ruled out the development of representative machinery capable of limiting the power of the monarch and the bureaucracy as in Great Britain.

The relations between monarch and administration in Prussia changed in the nineteenth century: the police state was replaced by a state of laws *(Rechtsstaat)* that carried over certain features of its predecessor. The administration henceforth worked within the framework of a system of laws. As Otto Mayer, the leading theorist of this form of constitutional government puts it, "A state whose administration does not act according to legal and duly documented forms is not a *Rechtsstaat.* A state which does abide by the law and due process embodies the ideal of the *Rechtsstaat* to the extent that it adheres to these forms and enforces their effect."[38] Mayer emphasizes the extent to which German law was modeled on French public law and thus makes clear what is similar in the French and German systems: in both cases it was administrative law that enabled the state to increase the degree of its autonomy from civil society. By contrast, in Great Britain administrative law was not highly developed, reflecting the limited development of the state itself.

With this in mind, it is easy to see how a state based on law and claiming to act in a rational, impartial, and functional manner could have seemed to Hegel the embodiment of Spirit.[39] Max Weber also based his thoughts on the German state in working out his model of bureaucracy. Both Hegel and Weber were fascinated by German "officialdom," which according to Jellinek had a profound influence on German public law: the bureaucratic state *(Beamtenstaat)* in Germany inevitably recalls certain fundamental features of the French political system. After 1871, under the new Reich, the Prussian administrative structure was extended to all of Germany. This could not help but increase still further the power of the top civil servants, who filled posts throughout the government. Bismarck chose his leading ministers from among this group. What is more, these ministers were not responsible to the Reichstag.

The German civil service therefore enjoyed a high degree of autonomy. It was protected by a body of strict administrative law, and its members were recruited on the basis of meritocratic criteria. Civil servants, the vast majority of whom were nobles, were thus able to infiltrate the political system, over which they have exercised an important influence right up to the present. From seventeenth-century Prussia to the German Federal Republic of today, top civil servants have always shared in the exercise of political power. If they ever held back from participation it was probably during the Weimar Republic, in which they could not see their place, somewhat like senior civil servants in France during the Third and perhaps also the Fourth Republic. The involvement of German senior civil servants in politics has been even greater than that of their French counterparts (so that Germany in this respect is the diametrical opposite of Great Britain). This involvement is reflected in the first comprehensive civil service law of 26 January 1937, according to which "the civil servant is responsible for carrying out the orders of the state, the embodiment of the National-Socialist Party" and "is obliged to render loyal service to the Führer and the Reich pursuant to the provisions of the public law." The General Federal Civil Service Law of 14 July 1953 states that the loyalty of the civil servant should be directed to the maintenance of "the fundamental democratic and liberal order." In contrast to French civil servants, who are obliged simply to abide by the provisions of public law, German civil servants are therefore required to uphold a political order, and this to some extent limits the differentiation of the state. By the same token the participation of German civil servants in political life at all levels is markedly greater than that of their counterparts in France, where in recent years only the highest-ranking civil servants have participated in politics, and even then only at the highest levels and only since the advent of Gaullism.

Educated primarily in the law,[40] German civil servants have carried their own values with them into the world of politics. This phenomenon, long ago criticized by Max Weber, accounts for the close identification of political power and administrative power. At present the civil servants make up the largest single group in the Bundestag, and a significant proportion of the members of the government are drawn from the ranks of the civil service.[41] Thus, as in France, a highly institutionalized state gives rise to a high level of participation by civil servants in political life. As representatives of a strong governmental power, senior civil servants in Germany, like their French counterparts, do not hesitate to accept jobs in private industry, where their contacts inside the administration can be put to good use.[42]

However, the German state is not as autonomous as the French state, as can be seen from the fact that the unity of elite groups is greater in Germany than in France. The French civil service is still almost entirely closed to outsiders, whereas nearly 50 percent of German senior civil servants worked in other professions before joining the civil service.[43] Thus the German bureaucracy is institutionalized only to a limited degree. What is more, German political parties play a far more important role in a civil servant's career than do French political parties: a man is more likely to advance rapidly to a higher-level post if he belongs to a political party. In some respects what we see in Germany is the development of a "party state," in which partisan political groups actually become state organs. Thus there is considerable osmosis between the top ranks of the civil service and the world of politics, besides which senior civil servants are often drawn from sectors of society outside the civil service in which they have previously made careers. As a result the German state has not achieved full autonomy and remains closely tied to civil society.

Similarly, in Italy and Spain the process that leads from the development of a political center to the construction of an autonomous state remains incomplete. As everyone knows, Italian unification did not come about until late in the nineteenth century and was achieved by the intervention of the Piedmontese government, which had been subject to strong French influence (reflected in centralization, the creation of a civil service and a body of public law, etc.). A system that was still in the process of developing toward statehood was imposed by the Piedmont on all of Italy. But the resistance encountered was so strong that Italy has still not managed to establish a truly autonomous state. In contrast to the French state, the Italian state has been unable to overcome the power of the Church, which in a variety of ways still exerts influence on Italian politics. Nor has the Italian state freed itself from the grip of the political parties, particularly the Christian Democratic Party, which exerts its influence on the government from within. All the political parties control certain private fiefdoms within the state and can appoint loyal civil servants as they please. This parallel government *(sottogoverno)* greatly limits the institutionalization of the state. Clientele relations also make their influence felt throughout the government, and their persistence is one sign of the lack of differentiation of the state from civil society. This lack of differentiation makes the rationalization of the state impossible and prevents the government from escaping the influence of certain special interests.[44]

8   Government by Civil Society: The Weakness of the Bureaucracy

The Weak-State Model: Great Britain

If the French state is regarded as the ideal type of *the*
state, then Great Britain must be viewed as the prime example of government by civil society, the state there being minimal. In Britain, allegiance
to the central government came about very early, and the cohesiveness
of the society was such that the country saw no attempts at secession like
those that recurred in France for many years to come. English unity
dates from before the Norman conquest, so that the Normans had only
to complete the process of centralization and extend administrative
practices to which the populace was already accustomed. What the Normans did of course was to divide English territory into five thousand
manors to be distributed to those who had followed William the Con-
queror. England therefore never experienced anything like the feudalism
that was to emerge on the continent. The Normans allowed the Anglo-
Saxons to maintain their customs and to continue a limited form of
self-government on the regional level, thereby preventing the formation
of subsystems that might have been tempted to claim independence
from the central government. Rather than try to dominate the periphery
via the stewardship of an outside administration *(intendants* or *Landräte),*
the central government used nonprofessional volunteers who already resided in the places they were to administer. Representative institutions,
universities, and juries all bear witness to civil society's capacity to
organize itself. Provincial notables and later the middle classes took part
in the activities of the central government. Parliament "gradually took
shape as an instrument capable of smoothing over conflicts and coordinating the activities of authorities that held one another in mutual esteem:
the king, the church, the barons, and certain classes of the people such
as the squires and the knights."[1] This gradual mixing of the various social
categories made it possible to achieve a national constitution without
forcible state intervention. Peripheral elites therefore elected not to

destroy the central authorities in order to achieve their own autonomy but rather to control the government through Parliament.[2] From the Magna Carta ("no taxation without representation"– 1215) to the revolution of 1688, the parliamentary principle came slowly to the fore and thus forestalled the development of an absolute monarchy of the type that emerged during this same period in France and Spain and that dominated the state-building process in those two countries. As Kantorowicz has shown, the body of the nation was epitomized in the body of the king. Parliament, as the representative of civil society, prevented the executive power from acquiring too much strength.[3] Magistrates and other local officials were recruited among the notables and not from the ranks of a local bureaucracy, so that the central government was not obliged to fill the ranks of the local bureaucracy with its own loyal agents. Since there was some degree of consensus as well as clearly demarcated natural borders, the state was not forced to dismantle existing communities to create administrative subdivisions, as the French government was forced to do when it set up the *généralités* and *départements*.

During the seventeenth century, at a time when absolute monarchies on the continent were establishing extensive bureaucracies, there were very few professional administrators in Charles I's England.[4] The men who worked for the king were mainly amateurs, which does not mean that they were not highly competent at what they did. For a long time the English central government had no military bureaucracy either. The first standing army in England came into being well after the French and Prussian armies. Freed of the necessity to wage internal war and protected by the sea against the strong states on the continent, England relies for its defense mainly on the Royal Navy. Furthermore, since social cohesiveness was assured largely by representative government and fusion of the various social classes, a centrally controlled police force was never deemed necessary. The level of professionalization of the police was for a long while quite low, and the police always stood aloof from politics. The total decentralization of the police force is one more sign of the difference between the British political system and the French or Prussian system, since in the latter two countries the police exercised tight central control over the full extent of the national territory.[5]

Clearly, then, the British central government did not establish the kind of bureaucratic apparatus necessary to bring about the transformation of what was merely a political center into a state, in the sense we are using the term. What is more, Britain lacked a body of administrative law that might have helped to mark off the boundaries between state and civil society. The influence of Rome on England was slight. Britain adhered to the tradition of common rather than Roman law, the body of common law being an outgrowth of civil society itself. Common law relies on a strict set of procedural rules and is based essentially on precedent rather than on a formal code. It rejects the distinction between private and public law and grants the state almost no special prerogatives as the embodiment of public power. At the local level the "rule of law" is assured by justices of the peace, mainly volunteers, and administrative courts are largely unknown. Juries are made up of ordinary citizens.

At the end of the nineteenth century Dicey remarked that "the system of administrative law and the principles on which it is based are undoubtedly foreign to the spirit and traditions of British institutions." It is true that in recent years special courts have been established to sit in judgment on acts of the administration in the areas of insurance, transportation, health, and the like, but the laws these courts enforce are the general laws of the land and except for the chief judge none of the members are paid and none are employed as civil servants.[6] Thus the difference between English law, which accords no privilege to the state, and the French, German, or Spanish legal systems, all of which include a body of administrative law, is easy to see.[7] Why does the political center in England lack the features characteristic of certain continental states? Because in Great Britain it was unnecessary for the political center to push for autonomy and to differentiate itself from civil society. Britain is ruled not by a state but by a social class, an "establishment," in association with the middle classes and the local gentry. This ruling class includes both the aristocracy (which never enjoyed the tax advantages and other privileges of the French nobility) and the bourgeoisie. Not only was it possible for members of the aristocracy to participate in business activities without derogating from nobility, it was also a rather simple matter for members of the bourgeoisie to mingle with the nobility and negotiate agreements of common interest to both parties. A true state was prevented from coming into being in part by the social mobility that occurred at the center, in part too by the mechanisms of representative government that were available. The development of the state in Great Britain has been minimal from the seventeenth century down to the present. It might be said that the state in England is a rather backward one, without intending to give an evolutionary connotation to the term "backward."[8]

Whereas in other countries such as France and Germany it was economic backwardness that led to the creation of a strong state, in Great

Britain it was the very rapid growth of capitalism and the market that resulted in the backwardness of the state, with civil society maintaining its position of dominance. Thus Britain never resorted to a mercantilist economic policy of the sort adopted by France and Prussia. State intervention in the economy was rendered useless by adherence to the maxim of *laissez-faire, laissez-passer*, economic individualism, and the market mechanism. For many years the development of any sort of economic administration in Great Britain was quite limited, and even today Britain has fewer nationalized firms than France. The only role of the state was to provide a navy to open up foreign markets. Its internal role was limited. In Great Britain the market reigns supreme, not the state. By contrast, in France and Prussia it was the state that organized the market. "Great Britain was the least mercantilist of the great powers and yet the first to industrialize."[9]

The ability of civil society to govern itself not only fostered the development of the market but also encouraged reliance on representative forms of government, thereby making a strong state unnecessary. This explains why no civil service developed in Great Britain until the end of the nineteenth century, in contrast to what took place in France, Prussia, and Spain. Until relatively recently, British civil servants were amateurs drawn from the privileged strata of society, men who attended first one of the public schools and later Oxford or Cambridge, where they picked up a smattering of the humanities but little in the way of economics or science.[10] The administration managed for quite a while to make do without full-time paid professional civil servants. Not until the reforms that followed the Northcote-Trevelyan report of 1854 were competitive examinations used for recruitment. In a similar vein, the central government preferred to rely on temporary special commissions rather than a permanent bureaucracy. Then, too, public corporations performed functions that on the Continent were usually left to departments of the state bureaucracy. These corporations belonged to the private sector and merely cooperated with the public authorities. This helped to limit the growth of the bureaucracy. These various factors help to explain the small size of the British bureaucracy,[11] a feature that makes Great Britain totally different from various strong-state continental systems.[12] It is of course true that a civil service has developed in Britain since the end of the nineteenth century. As recently as 1968, however, the Fulton report denounced the amateurism of this civil service and suggested taking inspiration, rather belatedly, from the French model by establishing, for instance, a civil service college.[13] Despite the various reforms that have been instituted, civil servants still enjoy no statutory protection and serve in theory at the pleasure of the monarch, though in reality their job security is quite high (note, too, that police officers, officials of the local administration, secondary school teachers, and university professors are not considered to be part of the civil service).[14]

Because British civil servants are not seen as the primary agents of an all-powerful state, they play little if any role in politics and only rarely move from government into private business. Unlike their French and German colleagues, they are in fact excluded from power[15] and are quite marginal as a segment of the ruling class.[16] The civil service is supposed to be completely neutral, as the *Manual of the Civil Service* makes plain. Since the Act of Establishment of 1907, any member of the civil service who wishes to run for office must resign, and he cannot hope for reinstatement should he lose the election. By contrast, in France a senior civil servant can serve as a deputy while retaining his right to return to the ranks of the civil service if he is beaten in some future election. Such practices are not allowed in Great Britain, where the cleavage between the administration and politics is virtually absolute.[17] Hence there are practically no senior civil servants in the British Parliament (in contrast to the Bundestag) or in the government (in contrast to France). On the other hand, businessmen, who along with the rest of the "establishment" have always been at the center of the British political system, are strongly represented in Parliament,[18] whereas business representation in the French, German, and Italian parliaments is quite insignificant. While there is a good deal of mobility between the world of politics and the world of business,[19] civil servants do not participate in this partial sharing of powers, which is so characteristic of the British, and to a lesser extent also of the American, political system. In certain countries on the Continent, the power of the state is reflected in the fact that senior civil servants play a key role in governing civil society, acting in both the economic and political spheres. By contrast, in Britain, where the political center did not develop into a true state because civil society proved capable of governing itself, and the relatively small number of civil servants, many of them poorly trained, play no role in either politics or the management of the market economy. Here again only history can account for the way in which power is either shared or fragmented.

The American Case

What radically distinguishes the United States from many European countries is the absence of a feudal past. Hence the United States was not forced, in order to become a nation, either to abolish great feudal estates or to wage war against an aristocracy of one sort or another. Before the United States became a nation it did not harbor a multitude of autonomous powers, hence it had no need of a state to crush those powers.[20]

In fact the American colonists had brought with them from England the principles later embodied in the Declaration of Independence and the Declaration of the Rights of Man—those from the Magna Carta that guaranteed equality before the law, strong representative institutions, limitations on the power of the executive, and a presumption in favor of selecting local officials by election. As in Great Britain, American society came into being with experience of self-government. The contractual basis of American society can be seen very clearly in the work of the Constitutional Convention of 1787. The individual state assemblies debated the merits of the new Constitution before agreeing to accept it and its guarantee of states' rights to the members of the Confederacy. Thus the nation was not put together by the actions of a central government. Quite the contrary: the nation was organized without the aid of anything remotely resembling the French state.

The modernization of the United States followed a course profoundly different from that of France and Prussia, where powerful states exerted fundamental influence from the seventeenth century on. What is more, there was less centralization in the United States than in Britain, where some degree of centralization was achieved quite early. Although the United States did take over a good many British institutions, it refused to allow the establishment of a central government with powers analogous to those the British government had enjoyed for many years. America was vehemently opposed to the notion of a sovereign state and long remained hostile to any increase in the power of the executive branch. Americans even argued against the theory that parliament is the sovereign representative of the will of the people.[21] In the United States, sovereignty is divided, power is shared. As in the systems of Montesquieu and Locke, not only is there separation of powers, but, too, the various functions of government are shared among a number of different institutions. This made it possible to modernize the system without concentrating all authority in one place.[22]

Having come into being without the aid of a state, "the first new nation"[23] based its legitimacy on a combination of the principles of liberty and equality, which served to strengthen a certain individualistic bias and to legitimate inequality of condition among the citizens, since such inequality was seen as resulting from an ostensible equality of opportunity. This accounts for Darwin's influence in the United States and for the prevalence of the myth of the "self-made man." The idea of the "survival of the fittest" was accepted, and the entrepreneur became a hero of the new society. These elitist theories provided a rationale for the wielding of power by a minority. In a society at once democratic, "open," and elitist, it was easy to see the state as a useless tyrant. Furthermore, the idea of a natural aristocracy resulting from the inherent inequalities among men of varying talent and ability was congenial to the Puritan cast of mind, which exerted great influence in the United States. Once again Protestantism served to reinforce individualism and therefore worked against the emergence of a state.[24]

Legitimate power was therefore wielded not by a state but rather by the elite groups that organized American society. Among these, the economic elite played a key role from the first: it exerted a strong influence on the writing of the Constitution[25] and played a prominent role in the political parties and in politics generally. Thus the power of the business community prevented the state from acquiring any real autonomy from the nineteenth century down to the present. As in Great Britain, there are large numbers of businessmen in both Congress and the Cabinet: many politicians were first either businessmen or lawyers.[26] But the lawyers who become politicians in America are not to be confused with the provincial *avocats* who once formed the backbone of most French political parties and represented the provinces in Paris. Lawyers who become politicians in the United States are almost always closely involved in the business world and are sometimes chosen directly by some large firm. Once elected, they serve as loyal spokesmen of the business community and continue to perform private legal services for many businesses while carrying out their public duties.[27] Ninety percent of Cabinet members from 1897 to 1973 have belonged to the social or economic elite. Seventeen percent of government employees, both civilian and military, worked in business before obtaining a post in government. Fifty-seven percent were lawyers with ties to major business firms. From the end of the nineteenth century to the present, nearly 80 percent of Cabinet members had close relations with the business community.[28]

Thus the business community has substantial influence in most public institutions. It also dominates the departments and agencies of the executive branch that control energy policy, trade policy, and foreign policy. Federal agencies responsible for supervising various sectors of the economy are usually staffed by personnel drawn from the very sectors they are supposed to regulate.[29] In other words, the business community has successfully penetrated the political system.

It is corresponsdingly more difficult for the political system to stand up to outside pressure, since it has never become fully institutionalized and has put off the task of establishing a true bureaucracy. It should be noted, too, that the choice of a federal system has served to reinforce the power of the individual states at the expense of the central government. Federalism distinguished the American model from both the French model of absolute *étatisation* and the British model of centralization. In the American political system the states are not mere agents of the central government but rather organs of distinct political entities, separate from and in many respects independent of the federal government.[30] The purview of the latter is therefore strictly limited. This explains why the federal bureaucracy for so long remained vulnerable and failed to achieve a significant degree of autonomy. Not until the Pendleton Act of 1883 was there any attempt to do away with the spoils system, under which civil servants were completely subservient to the political parties, making illusory any notion of an institutionalized state. The merit system, which developed slowly in the wake of the act and instituted compulsory examinations for civil service personnel, may be viewed as a consequence of the rapid growth of the United States after the Civil War and the concomitant extension of federal services. Similarly, the advent of the welfare state led to the creation of numerous federal agencies both to dispense services and to monitor other agencies and social problems at the grass roots.

Nevertheless, a fully autonomous and professionalized federal bureaucracy was slow to develop and met with considerable hostility which ended its development prematurely. Under Franklin Roosevelt there was a substantial return to the spoils system, and many senior civil servants lost their jobs to newcomers chosen for partisan political reasons. The merit system was in fact for many years applied only to the lower echelons of the civil service.[31] The lack of an institutionalized bureaucracy also meant that civil servants enjoyed no job security comparable to that of civil servants in France and Germany. As in Britain and Switzerland, the link between the civil service and the administration is tenuous. Furthermore, as in Britain, there is no substantial body of administrative law, which has not been necessary because of the limited degree of state autonomy. Similarly, there is no system of specialized administrative courts. It is also worthy of note that the United States took over the British system of common law, though not without certain initial doubts.[32]

The American administration today does not work in a vacuum isolated from civil society but maintains close relations with outside social, economic, and political groups.[33] These relations are similar to the clientele relations one finds in Italy, whose political system followed a quite different pattern of development. As we already noted, relations between the business community and the government in the United States have always been particularly close, and businessmen have infiltrated all levels of the federal bureaucracy.[34] It is a fact that many high-ranking civil servants began their careers in the private sector, particularly in the world of business, as is the case also in Germany and Switzerland. Thirty-six percent of federal bureaucrats are recruited from the public service sector, 24 percent from the business community, and 36 percent among lawyers, many of whom have close ties with the business community[35] and a majority of whom return to the private sector after a stint in government.[36]

Infiltrated by businessmen, the political system has never achieved true autonomy or carved out a specific niche of its own. This makes it clear why theorists of the "power elite" such as C. Wright Mills never paid any attention to government bureaucracy, which plays such a crucial role in other political systems. Senior civil servants in the United States are insecure in their posts and vulnerable to the influence of the business community and to partisan political pressures. Their participation in politics has been illegal ever since the 1949 Hatch Act, which, as in Great Britain, obliges any civil servant who wishes to run for political office to resign, without hope of reinstatement. Thus Britain and the United States, in contrast to France and Germany, maintain a strict separation between administrative and political personnel. There are virtually no civil servants in Congress. Relations between politics and bureaucracy in the other direction are quite different, however: there is constant political pressure on the bureaucracy in the United States, which is not the case in Britain.

Except for certain factors peculiar to the United States such as federalism, clientelism, and an individualism hostile to all forms of centralized power, to name a few, there is thus a certain similarity between the British and American political systems. In both cases the relative weakness of the state and the relatively low level of state autonomy and institutionalization reinforce the role played by the business community and the market. Although the federal government has in some areas grown rapidly and achieved some degree of institutionalization (with more and more civil servants recruited competitively and remaining in government throughout their careers),[37] the American state remains backward when compared with its French or German counterpart. Like the British system, the American political system does not claim to govern all aspects of civil society. It is in this sense that the state in America remains an "incomplete conquest."[38]

The State and Consociational Democracy

Since the 1960s the term "consociational democracy" has been used to describe political systems in which conflicts are resolved through negotiation and groups with different points of view settle their differences in a spirit of toleration and compromise rather than by application of the principle of majority rule. Such systems are found in societies with deep religious or ethnic divisions, as a result of which the number of opposing political groups is large. Although class differences may sometimes cut across the other cleavages in these societies, by and large the political dividing lines are other than class-based. Switzerland and the Netherlands, for example, have gradually developed a "policy of accommodation" that has made it possible to keep peace among groups strongly opposed to one another in fundamental ways. This sort of "vertical pluralism," arising from the existence of a number of cultures within a single social system, requires equal representation of all groups as the only possible way of avoiding total breakdown. "Good fences make good neighbors" seems an appropriate maxim to apply to this sort of system.[39] The fences in question are of course internal to the political systems in question and are in this sense to be distinguished from international borders.

The very fact that distinct "fences" continue to separate different groups within consociational systems, even after the political system has been established, makes clear how different such societies are both from centralized but stateless societies such as Great Britain and from highly centralized and "statized" societies such as France. The latter two types of society are not compatible with ethnic, religious, or linguistic divisions. Centralization and *"étatisation"* run counter to "organized pluralism." By contrast, in Switzerland there is neither a true center to the political system nor a true state. As Lijphart puts it, "If a society is divided by sharp, mutually reinforcing cleavages with each segment of the population living in its own separate world, the dangers of a breakdown of the system are clear." Accommodation, then, is nothing other than the "ability to make a pragmatic success from a theoretical impossibility."[40]

Such a society is neither homogeneous like Britain nor differentiated and atomized like France, where the citizen is supposed to give his allegiance to the state. Since there is no real center or state, peripheral allegiances are perfectly acceptable and legitimate. Social cohesiveness is thus not assured by the society itself, nor is it the state that runs civil society. This job falls instead to the various groups defined by the fundamental social cleavages. The model is clearly inapplicable to countries such as Ireland, where no accommodation has been possible. Consociational systems require the existence of a consensus within their constituent groups; each group must identify with its leaders and allow them the necessary flexibility to achieve accommodation with the other groups.[41] Hence individuals in consociational systems probably do not identify with society as a whole or with the state or with the social classes that cut across the various religious or ethnic groups by which they apparently feel fully represented.[42]

The consociational democracy model has often been applied to Switzerland,[43] even though direct democracy and a system of majority rule have sometimes been employed there to the detriment of accommodational politics and even though some of the divisions in Swiss society cut across one another. The religious dividing line does not coincide precisely with the linguistic dividing line, for instance. In order to understand how such a social system came about, we must again study its history. Unlike France, Switzerland never developed a state that claimed to have the right to settle social conflicts from without.

Once again, geography exerted a strong influence on the structure of the political system. With its mountainous terrain and many isolated valleys, Switzerland is a compartmentalized country in which there is a natural tendency for each city and valley to govern itself. A congeries of duchies, counties, bishoprics, cities, and cantons located at one extremity of the Holy Roman Empire was able to preserve its autonomy and thus to prevent the development of a centralized state. What is more, this was an area where trade was intense, so that a relatively large number of cities grew wealthy and strong and no single one among them could claim to be the center of such a highly pluralistic system. But since the Swiss valleys were surrounded by great powers that threatened their independence, in 1291 they signed a permanent pact of alliance and mutual aid. Thus the political system was the result not of a central state dominating its peripheries but rather of an association. Although these treaties were sometimes violated, resulting in civil war, they nevertheless account for the uniqueness of the Swiss political system, which was able to maintain a pluralist confederation during and after the religious wars.

On the eve of the French Revolution, Switzerland still had no central government.[44] But the influence of French political institutions gave rise at that time to some measure of centralization, accompanied by an expansion of the market, an end to some internal tolls, and encouragement of industry and commerce. The triumph of liberalism favored the bourgeoisie and made necessary a unification that was supported mainly by Protestants and feared by Catholics.[45] Thus the constitution of 1848 was mainly the work of German, Protestant, liberal, and economically developed Switzerland. It did away with internal boundaries and gave birth to the Swiss nation. As William Martin has pointed out, "the federal constitution did not begin with an idea but with a need.... In the mid-nineteenth century economic unity was seen as a necessary condition for the continued existence of the Confederation. It was this necessity that gave rise to political unity, and it was the job of the unified political system to work toward economic unification."[46]

In this respect Switzerland may be compared with Great Britain: in both countries it was the demands of the market that made nation-building indispensable. Both differ from France and Germany, where the state set out deliberately to create a market. Furthermore, Switzerland, like England, established representative institutions that enabled society to govern itself, making the creation of a state necessary. In contrast to what occurred in Britain, however, the economic unification of Switzerland did not strengthen the central authorities. Centralization took place without really affecting the pluralism of the political system. The various compromises and agreements between the different social groups (which were also ethnic, religious, and linguistic groups) survived. The continuing weakness of the state is therefore easy to understand.

Unlike France and Prussia but again like Great Britain, Switzerland was late to establish a standing army. Although military legislation is today a national affair, the enforcement of the law in peacetime is left up to the cantons. The cantons maintain tight control over the educational system. In general it may be said that the federal bureaucracy usually leaves the execution of laws up to the cantons. Thus Switzerland, like Britain, has no officials comparable to the French prefects constantly supervising the actions of the peripheral authorities. One further similarity with Britain is that the central government bureaucracy is still of modest size compared with the bureaucracies of countries with strong states.

The development of the central administration in Switzerland began in 1848, at a time when development of the French bureaucracy had already been underway for several centuries. Between that time and the present there has been only modest growth of the civil service, with most civil servants employed by the cantons.[47] Civil servants have no real legal status in Switzerland. They are not appointed for life as in France and Germany but rather for four-year terms, and some are not rehired when their term of office expires. In this respect Swiss civil servants resemble their British counterparts, who serve at the pleasure of the monarch. Although civil servants in both countries normally are assured of relatively stable employment, their lack of tenure is one more sign of the low level of state institutionalization in the two places.

The civil service has been no more successful than the political system in differentiating itself from civil society or in achieving autonomy of action. Thirty-four percent of senior civil servants held positions in the business world before entering public service.[48] This type of recruitment is virtually unknown in France, where the almost total institutionalization of the state has led to the development of a highly autonomous bureaucracy. In the same vein, Swiss civil servants are not recruited solely on the basis of meritocratic criteria as required by the Weberian model. In practice, in order to take account of the country's linguistic, religious, and cultural pluralism, some effort is made to achieve balance in civil service recruitment so that all groups are appropriately represented. This shows the extent to which peripheral allegiances are taken into account and makes it clear why no true state is possible in Switzerland.

It should now be clear why Swiss civil servants are scarcely better represented in the Federal Assembly than are their counterparts in the House of Commons or the American Congress, as against the strong representation of civil servants in the Bundestag. Again as in Britain and the United States, a high proportion of Swiss deputies are drawn from the business community. In both Switzerland and Great Britain, moreover, a high percentage of the elected representatives hold seats on boards of directors in the private sector. Each Christian Democratic deputy holds an average of 6.2 board seats and each Radical deputy an average of 4.1 seats. The former are connected mainly with the smaller capitalist firms, the latter with the larger.[49]

As we have found repeatedly, in countries with a highly institutionalized and autonomous state, senior civil servants play a key role at one level or another of national political life, and the business community is rather poorly represented among elected officials (this is true of France, Germany, and Italy). By contrast, in countries having weak states in which one or more political centers have emerged, thereby allowing civil society to govern itself, senior civil servants take no part in politics but the business community plays a crucial role (in Great Britain, the United States, and Switzerland). Thus, even in countries having the same type of social system, the relation between the state and the market is not always the same.[50] The foregoing remarks will, we hope, have convinced the reader that the metaphoric description of the state as the loyal agent of business is no longer tenable, for it misses the essential point: the relations among the various ruling groups in a country depend to a large extent on whether that country is ruled by a state or by one or more political centers.

Conclusion

Wrongly viewed as the inevitable product of political development, the state should rather be understood as a unique phenomenon, an innovation developed within a specific geographical and historical context. The state was first conceived as a response to crises that afflicted several Western societies during the late Middle Ages. It hardly needs repeating that these crises were not of a kind that must necessarily manifest itself in every social system, nor were they as simple as all too many recent analysts seem to think. The state was a product neither of the rise of capitalism nor of the opening of new trade routes, let alone of the growth of industry. The state was not a mere effect of economic modernization, as many sociologists still argue. A more correct characterization would be the following: the state was the political response that some European societies were forced to make to an increasing division of labor coupled with strong resistance to social change on the part of certain elements of feudal society; it was a way of reconciling the growing political incapacity of the great lords with the fact that they still maintained substantial control over economic and social life.

Under the circumstances the "state remedy" was in some ways rather paradoxical. By successfully putting forward claims to absolute autonomy, the state established itself by taking all political power away from the aristocracy. The state has been able to survive as long as it has undoubtedly because it proved capable of training its personnel, designing its institutions, elaborating a body of public law, and intervening in the economic life of the nation, often in order to satisfy its own needs. This was the price exacted by a social order that might be described as "hyperfeudalized." On the other hand, it will come as no surprise that state interference with the economy required constant compromise with the key elements of civil society, which, even if they were incapable of self-government, always proved capable of organizing to protect fundamental interests. First mercantilism and later state-orchestrated policies of industrialization had to take account of the survival of very powerful agricultural interests, whether controlled by the aristocracy or by the peasantry. Similarly, interventionist policies always had to be defined in the light of various bourgeois interests that succeeded one another historically. When all is said and done, the state's raison d'être may be seen to lie in the innovational dynamic imposed upon it by its own interests and by the inflexibility of civil society—a dynamic facilitated by the tendency toward structural differentiation inherent in the Western cultural code.

As a response to a specific crisis affecting one part of Europe and as the product of a specific culture, the state remedy is quite unlikely to prove satisfactory in third world societies faced with other problems and moved by other visions of the future. Africa and Asia are no longer blinded by the illusions of state building: the whole process has ceased to be regarded as a symptom of modernization and has come to be viewed as one of the more prominent causes of the failure to modernize as well as of the tensions and violence with which young nations are currently afflicted. As nonwestern cultures experience a reawakening, there is growing awareness that the political regime of the future will be a state in name only and that it must be based on new ideas, on innovations and adjustments comparable to those that postfeudal Europe was forced to undergo.

And what about that part of Europe in which the state was born? Do we not see signs of a different kind of crisis there? Do the issues of the past have anything in common with the issues of today? It must of course be allowed that the state formula has shown itself to be extremely flexible. Thanks to this flexibility the state has survived the period of industrialization, the awakening of the working class, and the rise of mass politics, and it has left its mark on whole periods of history, determining the course of events according to its own laws. Today, however, many signs seem to indicate that society has outgrown the state: separatist movements, the popularity of "self-management," and the crisis afflicting many state institutions all suggest that the once necessary monopoly of political power by the state has lost its raison d'être. Even more serious, perhaps, is the fact that the social rigidity against which the state once fought has begun to afflict the state itself, as the special interests the state was designed to destroy reassert themselves within its very bosom.

Paradoxically, it is in those societies in Europe and North America that once seemed able to get along without a state and to organize a system of self-government around a more or less solid political center that the state seems to have grown most in recent years. The United States has seen steadily increasing centralization and bureaucratization of late, while the Scandinavian countries and England have adopted systems of social protection and nationalization policies on a scale comparable to and sometimes even exceeding what we have seen in France. This has involved no fundamental upheavals, however: bureaucracy is still underdeveloped in Britain, the social and economic elites continue to play a crucial role, and British nationalization policy is highly flexible, following the vagaries of governmental change.

It would seem, in fact, that societies with minimal states, particularly Great Britain, are still capable of achieving an almost natural compatibility between social function and political function. The political function of the state has been based on an old tradition of safeguarding individual and collective liberties, as is shown by the early development in England of a theory of national sovereignty and by the long-standing tradition of habeas corpus. In contrast, societies on the continent with strong states have been struggling for several decades with the dangers of political destabilization due to the breakdown of the state model. This very likely accounts for the success of fascism and Nazism in these countries, a success that nullified the legal guarantees that the state had developed, practiced, and promulgated.

On one point there is no room for doubt: although the state undoubtedly served as an instrument of political rationalization, it has not been the only such instrument and is having more and more difficulties in fulfilling this role. While it has proved an effective remedy in certain crisis situations, the state is not necessarily capable of dealing with every issue. Hence it is wrong to look upon the state as the only way of governing societies in all times and all places.

Afterword

The purpose of this book is to clarify the concept of the state. Because this concept has frequently been applied, without theoretical justification, to every imaginable kind of political system, its heuristic value for contemporary political analysis has to some extent been dissipated. Though it is rare to find a clear definition of just what is meant by "the state," the term is commonly used [in what has come to be called "modernization theory"] to denote the political structure that results from a lengthy process of centralization, a process that is more or less explicitly said to be governed by a general law of social evolution common to all societies.

If, however, we turn from modernization theory to social theory as such, we find that social theorists have generally taken a narrower view of the state. Disregarding the differences between the various theoretical traditions within sociology, we can state that, in all of these traditions, a clear distinction is made between "the state" and the "political center" of society. Because this distinction depends on the idea of "social differentiation," the sociological concept of the state is not only more precise but also more operational than the concept of the state found in modernization theory.

In these circumstances the writer who wishes to treat the concept of the state faces a dilemma: either he must settle for a broad and therefore largely useless definition of the state or he must concede that "the state" is not a universal concept but rather the product of a specific historical crisis to which different premodern societies are vulnerable in different degrees. Hence it is no longer possible to maintain that states are found everywhere. On the other hand, we do not wish to argue that the state is peculiar to a single country or even to a small number of countries. Our point is simply this: in each society, particular historical processes foster state building to a greater or lesser degree.

This book was written at a time when a need was felt, particularly in the English-speaking countries, to view the state in a historical light.

What was probably the most innovative work in political theory reflected this need. Today, the crisis in social theory is even broader than it was then, and the urge to consult history is even more widely shared. The crisis has also led some sociologists to turn back to more traditional forms of sociological analysis based on methodological individualism or simple empirical approaches. Much of this work is guided by purely normative considerations.

These developments have a great deal to do with the methodological problems inherent in historical sociology and with their attendant epistemological uncertainties. Simply to give up social theory, however, is not the most useful way to respond to these problems. In this book we have set ourselves the task of identifying various phases of the state building process and various relations between the rise of the state and the development of society. The sociology of the state should, we think, continue to make use of history, but it should be careful to avoid replacing an unsatisfactory form of evolutionary theory with yet another evolutionary theory based, this time, on politics and leading to the conclusion that once the state is established, its nature and form are determined and will never change. In particular, we think it would be useful to study the conditions under which one type of state is transformed into another.

July 1982

Notes

Chapter 1

1. Karl Marx, *A Contribution to the Critique of Political Economy* (New York: International Publishers, 1970), preface, p. 20.

2. Karl Marx, *Lettres à Kugelmann* (Paris: Editions Sociales, 1971), p. 30.

3. Karl Marx, "Critique of the Gotha Program," in *Marx and Engels: Basic Writings on Politics and Philosophy*, ed. Lewis S. Feuer (New York: Doubleday, 1959), p. 127.

4. See part 3 of this book.

5. Karl Marx, *Grundrisse*, trans. M. Nicolaus (New York: Vintage, 1973), p. 884.

6. Marx, "Critique of the Gotha Program," p. 128.

7. Karl Marx, collection of writings from the *Neue Rheinische Zeitung* published by Editions Sociales under the title *Nouvelle gazette rhénane*.

8. Concerning the state's claim to independence, see Pierre Birnbaum, *Les sommets de l'Etat* (Paris: Editions du Seuil, 1977), chap. 1. Translated by Arthur Goldhammer under the title *The Heights of Power* (Chicago: University of Chicago Press, 1982).

9. Karl Marx, *Critique of Hegel's 'Philosophy of Right,'* ed. Joseph O'Malley (Cambridge, England: Cambridge University Press, 1970; rev. ed., 1972), p. 11.

10. Ibid., p. 72.

11. Ibid., p. 46.

12. Ibid., p. 45.

13. Ibid., p. 48.

14. Ibid., p. 46.

15. Karl Marx, "On the Jewish Question," in *Early Writings*, ed. Tom Bottomore (New York: McGraw Hill, 1963), pp. 28–29.

16. Marx, *Critique of Hegel's 'Philosophy of Right,'* p. 49.

17. Ibid., p. 51.

18. Ibid., p. 44.

19. Cited by Eric Weil, *Hegel et l'Etat* (Paris: Vrin, 1950), p. 15.

20. Marx, *Critique of Hegel's 'Philosophy of Right,'* p. 100.

21. Marx, "Critique of the Gotha Program," p. 127.

22. John Maguire has given a remarkable account of these two aspects of Marx's work. His book is the only thorough treatment of Marx's political theory. See John Maguire, *Marx's Theory of Politics* (Cambridge, England: Cambridge University Press, 1978), pp. 199ff. Concerning this point, see also Shlomo Avineri, *The Social and Political Thought of Karl Marx* (Cambridge, England: Cambridge University Press, 1968), chap. 2.

23. Karl Marx, *The Eighteenth Brumaire of Louis Bonaparte* (New York: International Publishers, 1963), p. 121.

24. Ibid., p. 118.

25. Ibid., p. 121.

26. Ibid., p. 122.

27. Ibid., p. 131.

28. Friedrich Engels, *The Origin of the Family, Private Property, and the State* (New York: International Publishers, 1942), p. 157.

29. Alain Rouquié, "L'hypothèse 'bonapartiste' et l'émergence des systèmes politiques semi-compétitifs," *Revue française de science politique,* December 1975, p. 109.

30. Karl Marx and Friedrich Engels, *The German Ideology* (New York: International Publishers, 1970), pp. 53, 68-69.

31. Marx, *The Eighteenth Brumaire,* p. 121.

32. Karl Marx, *La guerre civile en France:* First Draft (Paris: Editions Sociales, 1953), pp. 188-89.

33. Ibid., pp. 210-12 and 214.

34. Claude Lefort, *Eléments d'une critique de la bureaucratie* (Geneva: Droz, 1971), pp. 289-92.

35. Marx, *The Eighteenth Brumaire,* p. 123.

36. Karl Marx, *The Civil War in France* (New York: International Publishers, 1940), p. 56.

37. Engels, *The Origin,* pp. 156-57.

38. Marx and Engels, "The Communist Manifesto," in *Basic Writings,* p. 9.

39. Maguire, *Marx's Theory of Politics,* pp. 24-26.

40. Friedrich Engels, *Anti-Dühring* (New York: International Publishers, 1939), p. 307.

41. Engels, *The Origin,* p. 158.

42. See Maurice Godelier, "La notion de 'mode de production antique' et les schémas marxistes d'évolution des sociétés," *Cahiers du Centre d'Etude et de Recherche Marxistes.* Henri Lefebvre has also called attention to the different approaches to the state that may be found in Marx's work: see Lefebvre's *De l'Etat* (Paris: Union Generale d'Edition, 1976), vol. 1, chap. 7. He is also one of the few present-day

Marxists to take seriously the diversity of modern state forms (see ibid., 1:99).

43. Emile Durkheim, *Textes* (Paris: Editions de Minuit, 1975), 3:170.

44. Emile Durkheim, *Leçons de sociologie* (Paris: Presses Universitaires de France, 1950), p. 8.

45. Emile Durkheim, *Montesquieu et Rousseau* (Paris: Marcel Riviere, 1966), p. 36.

46. Concerning Durkheim's view of history, see Robert Bellah, "Durkheim and History," in Robert Nisbet, ed., *Emile Durkheim* (Englewood Cliffs, NJ: Prentice-Hall, 1965).

47. Emile Durkheim, *La science sociale et l'action*, ed. Jean-Claude Filloux (Paris: Presses Universitaires de France, 1970), p. 202.

48. Durkheim, *Leçons de sociologie*, p. 58.

49. Durkheim, *Textes*, 3:238. See also pp. 257 and 263.

50. Emile Durkheim, *De la division du travail social* (Paris: Presses Universitaires de France, 1960). Cited here from George Simpson's English translation: *The Division of Labor in Society*, p. 222.

51. Ibid., pp. 199–200 (Eng. trans., p. 221).

52. Ibid., p. 198 (Eng. trans., p. 219).

53. Ibid., p. 200.

54. Ibid.

55. Durkheim, *Leçons de sociologie*, pp. 95–96.

56. Durkheim, *De la division du travail social*, p. 205. See Jean-Claude Filloux, *Durkheim et le socialisme* (Geneva: Droz, 1977), chap. 6.

57. Durkheim, *Leçons de sociologie*, pp. 111–13.

58. See for example Melvin Richter, "Durkheim's Politics and Political Theory," in Kurt Wolff, ed., *Emile Durkheim, Essays on Sociology and Philosophy* (London, 1964), p. 172. See also Victor Karady, "Durkheim, les sciences sociales et l'Université: bilan d'un semi-échec," *Revue française de sociologie,* April–June 1976.

59. Durkheim, *Leçons de sociologie*, p. 77.

60. Ibid., p. 71.

61. Ibid., p. 61.

62. Durkheim, *Textes*, 3:210.

63. See the article "L'Etat" in Durkheim, *Textes*, vol. 3. See also the article "Débat sur le rapport entre les fonctionnaires et l'Etat" in the same volume.

64. Ibid., p. 177.

65. Karl Marx, "La loi sur les vols de bois," *Œuvres philosophiques* (Costes, 1937), 5:135.

66. See Pierre Birnbaum, "La conception durkheimienne de l'Etat; l'apolitisme des fonctionnaires," *Revue française de sociologie*, April–June 1976.

67. Durkheim, *De la division du travail social* (Eng. trans., p. 28).

68. Emile Durkheim, *Le suicide* (Paris: Presses Universitaires de France, 1960), p. 448.

69. Alexis de Tocqueville, *L'ancien régime et la révolution* (Paris: Gallimard, 1952), p. 85.

70. See Robert Nisbet, *The Sociological Tradition* (London: Heinemann, 1966), and Pierre Birnbaum, *Sociologie de Tocqueville* (Paris: Presses Universitaire de France, 1969), chap. 7.

71. According to Durkheim, "if one class of society is obliged, in order to live, to take any price for its services, while another can abstain from such action thanks to resources at its disposal which, however, are not necessarily due to any social superiority, the second has an unjust advantage over the first at law." *De la division du travail social*, p. 378 (Eng. trans., p. 384).

72. Anthony Giddens, "Durkheim's Political Sociology," in *Studies in Social and Political Theory* (London: Hutchinson, 1977), p. 269.

73. Hans Gerth and C. Wright Mills, eds., *From Max Weber* (New York: Oxford University Press, 1958), p. 47.

74. Anthony Giddens, *Capitalism and Modern Social Theory* (Cambridge, England: Cambridge University Press, 1971), p. 234.

75. Max Weber, *Wirtschaft und Gesellschaft* (Tübingen: J. C. B. Mohr, 1976), chap. 3, sec. 10, pp. 140ff.

76. Ibid., chap. 3, sec. 14, pp. 157–58.

77. See Max Weber, *On Charisma and Institution Building*, ed. Shmuel Eisenstadt (Chicago: University of Chicago Press, 1968).

78. Weber, *Wirtschaft und Gesellschaft*, chap. 3, sec. 6, p. 130.

79. Ibid., chap. 3, sec. 5, p. 128.

80. Max Weber, "Bureaucracy," *From Max Weber*, p. 211. Concerning the appearance of a developmentalist conception in Weber's work, see Reinhard Bendix, *Max Weber: An Intellectual Portrait* (London: Methuen, 1966), pp. 387ff.

81. Weber, *Wirtschaft und Gesellschaft*, chap. 1, sec. 17, p. 29.

82. Weber, *From Max Weber*, p. 83.

83. Weber, "Bureaucracy," *From Max Weber*, pp. 204ff.

84. Weber, *Wirtschaft und Gesellschaft*, chap. 3, sec. 5, p. 129.

85. See for example Peter Blau, "Weber's Theory of Bureaucracy," in Dennis Wrong, ed., *Max Weber* (Englewood Cliffs, NJ: Prentice-Hall, 1970); and Martin Albrov, *Bureaucracy* (London: Macmillan, 1970), chap. 3.

86. Max Weber, "Capitalism and Rural Society in Germany," *From Max Weber*, p. 373.

87. In this respect, Weber was far more critical of bureaucracy than most other German theorists of the turn of the century. See David Beetham, *Max Weber and the Theory of Modern Politics* (London:

Allen and Unwin, 1974), pp. 19ff and chap. 6. The author gives a very pertinent analysis of Weber's historical writings.

88. Ibid., p. 199.

89. Weber, *From Max Weber*, p. 95.

90. Ibid., article on "Bureaucracy."

91. Ibid., pp. 210–11.

92. Ibid., pp. 211–18.

93. Ibid., p. 385.

94. Ibid., p. 232.

Chapter 2

1. Pierre Birnbaum, *La fin du politique* (Paris: Seuil, 1975); Gianfranco Poggi, *The Development of the Modern State* (London: Hutchinson, 1978), p. 10.

2. Neil Smelser, "Toward a Theory of Modernization," in *Essays in Sociological Explanation* (Englewood Cliffs, NJ: Prentice-Hall, 1968).

3. Talcott Parsons, *Structure and Process in Modern Societies* (Glencoe, Ill.: The Free Press, 1960), p. 241.

4. Talcott Parsons, *The System of Modern Society* (Englewood Cliffs, NJ: Prentice-Hall, 1971), p. 78.

5. Talcott Parsons, "Evolutionary Universals in Society," *American Journal of Sociology*, June 1964.

6. Alvin Gouldner, *The Coming Crisis of Western Sociology* (London: Heinemann, 1970), p. 347.

7. Talcott Parsons, *Societies: Evolutionary and Comparative Perspectives* (Englewood Cliffs, NJ: Prentice-Hall, 1966).

8. Ibid., pp. 146–47.

9. Parsons, *The System of Modern Society*, p. 31.

10. Ibid., p. 71.

11. Ibid., p. 72.

12. Ibid., pp. 62ff.

13. See Shmuel Eisenstadt, *Modernization: Protest and Change* (Englewood Cliffs, NJ: Prentice-Hall, 1966), chaps. 1 and 2; *The Political Systems of Empires* (New York: Free Press, 1963), chaps. 1 and 2 and pp. 365–71; "Social Change, Differentiation, and Evolution," *American Sociological Review* 29, no. 3:375–86.

14. Shmuel N. Eisenstadt, "Some New Looks at the Problem of Relations between Traditional Societies and Modernization," *Economic Development and Cultural Change* 16, no. 3 (1968): 436–50.

15. Neil Smelser, "Mechanisms of Change and Adjustment to Change," in Bert Hoselitz and Wilbert Moore, eds., *Industrialization and Society* (United Nations Educational, Scientific and Cultural Organization in conjunction with Mouton, 1963), pp. 32–56.

16. Ibid.

17. Ibid., p. 44. Concerning the state's role in resolving conflicts, see also Kalman H. Silvert, ed., *Expectant People, Nationalism and Development* (New York: Random House, 1963), p. 19.

18. Smelser, "Mechanisms," pp. 51–52.

19. Wilbert Moore, "Industrialization and Social Change," in Hoselitz and Moore, eds., *Industrialization and Society*, p. 359.

20. Samuel P. Huntington, "Political Modernization: America Versus Europe," in Reinhard Bendix, ed., *State and Society* (Boston: Little, Brown, 1968), pp. 170–99.

21. On the definition of autonomy, see Shmuel N. Eisenstadt, *Social Differentiation and Stratification* (Glenview, IL: Scott, Foresman, 1971), p. 13.

22. For another definition of autonomy, cf. Fred Riggs, "The Idea of Development Administration," in Edward Weidner, ed., *Development Administration in Asia* (Chapel Hill, NC: Duke University Press, 1970), p. 34.

23. Eisenstadt, *Social Differentiation*, pp. 39–46.

24. Eisenstadt, *The Political Systems of Empires*, chap. 13.

25. Shmuel N. Eisenstadt, *Tradition, Change and Modernity* (New York: Wiley, 1973), chap. 13.

26. Samuel Finer, "State-Building, State Boundaries and Border Control," *Social Sciences Information* 13, nos. 4–5:86–87. As we shall see later on, it seems that for some reason Finer postdated the emergence of a centralized political system in England.

27. Cf. Finer, "State-Building" as well as "State and Nation-Building in Europe: The Role of the Military," in Charles Tilly, ed., *The Formation of National States in Western Europe* (Princeton: Princeton University Press, 1975), pp. 84–163.

28. Parsons, *Societies*, p. 114.

29. Cf. J. Peter Nettl, "The State as a Conceptual Variable," *World Politics*, July 1968, p. 562.

30. Cf. Reinhard Bendix, "Industrialization, Ideologies and Social Structure," in Amitai Etzioni and Eva Etzioni, eds., *Social Change* (New York: Basic Books, 1973).

31. Jürgen Habermas, *L'espace public* (French translation, Paris: Payot, 1978), p. 90 (first published in German in 1962).

32. Ibid., pp. 90ff.

33. On the importance of this distinctive feature, cf. Cyril Black, *The Dynamics of Modernization* (New York: Harper and Row, 1967), pp. 13ff, and Joseph Strayer, *Medieval Statecraft and the Perspectives of History* (Princeton: Princeton University Press, 1971).

34. Cf. Reinhard Bendix, *State and Society*, p. 71.

35. Nisbet, "State and Family," in *Social Change*, pp. 190–210.

36. Albert Hirschman, *Exit, Voice and Loyalty* (Cambridge: Harvard University Press, 1970).

37. Finer, "State and Nation-Building," pp. 80-82 and 98.

38. Ibid., p. 98. At this level of argument we find some of the fundamental points used by Rokkan in establishing his conceptual map of Europe.

39. On the particularistic significance of nationalism, see Anthony Douglas Smith, *Theories of Nationalism* (London: Duckworth, 1971), chap. 3.

40. See especially Bernard Guénée, *L'occident aux XIVe et XVe siècles: les Etats* (Paris: Presses Universitaires de France, 1974), and Joseph Strayer, *On the Medieval Origins of the Modern State* (Princeton: Princeton University Press, 1970), pp. 15-16 and 25. See also Carl J. Friedrich, *La démocratie constitutionelle* (Paris: Presses Universitaires de France, 1958), pp. 12-14.

41. Eisenstadt, *Social Differentiation*, p. 39.

42. Eisenstadt, *Modernization*, chap. 3.

43. Ibid. See also Eisenstadt, *Tradition, Change and Modernity*, pp. 40ff and 47ff.

44. Eisenstadt, *Tradition, Change and Modernity*, pp. 47ff.

45. Cf. Shmuel N. Eisenstadt, "Social Change, Differentiation and Evolution," *American Sociological Review* 29, no. 3 (1964): 375-86, and "Institutionalization and Change," *American Sociological Review* 29, no. 2 (1964).

46. Samuel P. Huntington, *Political Order in Changing Societies* (New Haven: Yale University Press, 1968), p. 9.

47. Ibid., p. 19.

48. Cf. Robert Robins, *Political Institutionalization and the Integration of Elites* (Beverly Hills: Sage Publication Papers, 1976), chaps. 1-3.

49. Concerning certain aspects of this problem, cf. Bert Hoselitz, "Levels of Economic Performance and Bureaucratic Structures," in Joseph La Palombara, ed., *Bureaucracy and Political Development* (Princeton: Princeton University Press, 1967), pp. 168-98.

50. Robert H. Lowie, *The Origin of the State* (New York, 1927).

51. Edward E. Evans-Pritchard and Meyer Fortes, *African Political Systems* (Oxford: Oxford University Press, 1940). For an introduction to other anthropological theories of the state, see Lawrence Krader, *Formation of the State* (Englewood Cliffs, NJ: Prentice-Hall, 1968), and Georges Balandier, *Anthropologie politique* (Paris: Presses Universitaires de France, 1978).

52. Eisenstadt, *The Political Systems of Empires*.

53. Reinhard Bendix, *Nation-Building and Citizenship* (New York: Wiley, 1964), p. 47.

54. Parsons, *Societies*, pp. 29ff.

55. Ibid., p. 110.

56. Parsons, *The System of Modern Societies*, p. 149.

57. For a critique of the reversion to a unilinear theory of development in Parsons, see G. Swanson, "Review of Parsons," *British Journal of Sociology* 3 (1973):390–92.

58. Gideon Sjoberg, *The Preindustrial City* (New York: The Free Press, 1965), chap. 8.

59. Numa-Denis Fustel de Coulanges, *La cité antique* (Paris: Hachette, 1879), pp. 151ff and 237ff.

60. Ibid., pp. 265ff, 283ff, and 325ff.

61. Claude Nicolet, *Le métier de citoyen dans la république romaine* (Paris: Gallimard, 1976), pp. 426–27 and Conclusion.

62. Eisenstadt, *Social Differentiation and Stratification*, pp. 101ff. See also *Tradition, Change and Modernity*, pp. 261ff. For a historian's contribution to the critical analysis of Chinese bureaucracy, see Etienne Balazs, *La bureaucratie céleste* (Paris: Gallimard, 1968).

63. See Thomas W. Arnold, *The Caliphate* (Oxford: Oxford University Press, 1924), pp. 189ff and Emile Tyan, "Notes sur la distinction du spirituel et du temporel dans le califat," *Annales de la Faculté de droit de Beyrouth* 1 (1951):5ff.

64. See Erwin Rosenthal, *Political Thought in Medieval Islam* (Cambridge: Cambridge University Press, 1958), pp. 112–17, and Bertrand Badie, "La philosophie politique de l'hellénisme musulman," *Revue française de science politique*, April 1977.

65. On the *eqta* see Claude Cahen, "Economy, Society and Institution," in P. M. Holt, Ann Lambton, and Bernard Lewis, eds., *The Cambridge History of Islam* (Cambridge: Cambridge University Press, 1970), vol. 2B, and Claude Cahen, "L'évolution de l'*eqta* du XIe au XIIe siècle," *Annales: Economies. Sociétés. Civilisations*, January–March 1953.

66. See especially Leonard Binder, *The Ideological Revolution in the Middle East* (New York: Wiley, 1964).

67. See Bertrand Badie, *Le développement politique* (Economica, 1978), pp. 50ff.

68. Edward Shils, *Political Development in the New States* (The Hague: Mouton, 1960), particularly the description of political democracy as the final stage of political development. See also Gabriel Almond and Bingham Powell, *Comparative Politics* (Boston: Little, Brown, 1966).

69. Lucian Pye, *Aspects of Political Development* (Boston: Little, Brown, 1967), pp. 5–10 and 62ff. The same general view may be found in Organski, who sees the nation-state as an essential phase of all political development: see Abramo F. K. Organski, *The Stages of*

Political Development (New York: Knopf, 1965). As we pointed out earlier, Samuel Huntington's development model is also apparently in many respects a faithful copy of the pattern of development of Western nation-states.

70. See Edward Shils, *Center and Periphery* (Chicago: University of Chicago Press, 1975).

71. Edward Shils, "On the Comparative Study of the New States," in Clifford Geertz, ed., *Old Societies and New States* (New York: Free Press, 1963).

72. On this point cf. the critiques of Kenneth Bock, "Theories of Progress and Evolution," in Werner Cahnman and Alvin Boskoff, eds., *Sociology and History* (New York: Free Press, 1964).

73. See Robert Nisbet, *Social Change and History* (New York: Oxford University Press, 1969), pp. 275ff.

74. On this point see Charles Tilly, "Clio et Minerve," published in French translation in Pierre Birnbaum and François Chazel, eds., *Théorie sociologique* (Paris: Presses Universitaires de France, 1975), p. 573.

75. Perry Anderson, *Lineages of the Absolutist State* (London: New Left Books, 1974).

76. Immanuel Wallerstein, *The Modern World System* (New York: Academic Press, 1974).

77. Guénée, *L'Occident aux XIVe et XVe siècles*, pp. 94ff.

78. Strayer, *On the Medieval Origins of the Modern States*, pp. 24-25.

79. On this point see Bendix, *Nation-Building and Citizenship*, pp. 41ff.

80. Ibid.

81. Ibid., pp. 7-8. See also Milton Singer, ed., *Traditional India: Structure and Change* (Austin: University of Texas Press, 1959).

82. Ernest Gellner, *Thought and Change* (Chicago: University of Chicago Press, 1965).

83. Clifford Geertz, *Agricultural Involution* (Berkeley: University of California Press, 1963), pp. 90ff.

84. Cf. Jürgen Habermas, *La technique et la science comme idéologie* (Paris: Gallimard, 1973); Giuseppe Di Palma, *Apathy and Participation* (New York: Free Press, 1970), and the remarks of Shmuel Eisenstadt himself in *Tradition, Change and Modernity*, pp. 238ff.

85. Gouldner, *The Coming Crisis of Western Sociology*, p. 359.

86. On this point see Anthony David Smith, *The Concept of Social Change* (London: Routledge and Kegan Paul, 1973), pp. 68ff.

87. Fred Riggs, *Administration in Developing Countries* (Boston: Houghton Mifflin, 1964), pp. 24ff.

88. Tilly, "Clio et Minerve," p. 580.
89. Geertz, *Agricultural Involution*, pp. 89ff.
90. Ibid., p. 95.
91. Shmuel N. Eisenstadt, "Breakdowns of Modernization," *Economic Development and Cultural Change* 12, no. 4:345-67.
92. Tilly, "Clio et Minerve," pp. 574-75.
93. Charles Petit-Dutaillis, *La monarchie féodale en France et en Angleterre*, 2d ed. (Paris: Albin Michel, 1971), pp. 126ff.
94. Amitai Etzioni, "The Epigenesis of Political Communities at the International Level," *American Journal of Sociology* January 1963, pp. 407-21.
95. See Norbert Elias, *La dynamique de l'Occident* (Paris: Calmann-Levy, 1975), first published in German in 1939, and Charles Tilly, "Reflections on the History of European State-Making," in Tilly, ed., *The Formation of National States in Western Europe*, pp. 25ff.
96. Etzioni, "The Epigenesis of Political Communities," pp. 409ff.
97. See Joan Davies, *Social Mobility and Political Change* (London: Macmillan, 1969), p. 97.
98. Habermas, *L'espace public*, pp. 149ff.
99. Habermas, *La technique*, p. 38.
100. Peter Bachrach and Morton Baratz, "Les deux faces du pouvoir," published in French translation in Pierre Birnbaum, ed., *Le pouvoir politique* (Paris: Dalloz, 1975), pp. 61-72; Steven Lukes, "La troisième dimension du pouvoir," published in French translation in ibid., pp. 73ff; and above all Claus Offe, "Structural Problems of the Capitalist State," *German Political Studies*, vol. 1 (Beverly Hills: Sage Publications, 1974), pp. 31ff.
101. Offe, "Structural Problems," p. 41.
102. Ibid., pp. 38ff.
103. Habermas, *L'espace public*, pp. 94ff, and *La technique*, p. 30.
104. Habermas, *La technique*, p. 42.
105. See Gino Germani, *Politique, société et modernisation* (Paris: Duculot, 1972), pp. 119-22 and 127-30.
106. Clifford Geertz, *The Interpretation of Cultures* (New York: Basic Books, 1973), p. 312.
107. As Eisenstadt himself acknowledges in *Tradition, Change and Modernity*, p. 15.
108. Shmuel N. Eisenstadt, "Varieties of Political Development: The Theoretical Challenge," in Shmuel N. Eisenstadt and Stein Rokkan, eds., *Building States and Nations* (Beverly Hills: Sage Publications, 1973), 1:42ff.
109. Otto Hintze, "The State in Historical Perspective," in Bendix, *State and Society*, pp. 155ff.

110. Geertz, *The Interpretation of Cultures*, p. 318.

111. On this subject see Bendix, *Nation-Building and Citizenship*, pp. 141ff.

112. J. Peter Nettl, *Political Mobilization* (London: Faber and Faber, 1967), pp. 76ff and 383ff.

113. Ibid., p. 80.

Introduction to Part 2

1. See especially Shils, *Center and Periphery*, and Rajni Kothari, "The Confrontations of Theories with National Realities," in Eisenstadt and Rokkan, eds., *Building States and Nations*, vol. 1.

2. It is possible to accept Charles Tilly's definition of the state: "An organization which controls the population occupying a defined territory is a state *in so far as* (1) it is differentiated from other organizations operating in the same territory; (2) it is autonomous; (3) it is centralized; and (4) its divisions are formally coordinated with one another." See Tilly, *The Formation of National States in Western Europe*, p. 70.

Chapter 3

1. Charles Tilly, *The Vendée* (Cambridge: Harvard University Press, 1964).

2. Ibid., chap. 9.

3. Ibid., chap. 4.

4. Ibid., chap. 13.

5. This analysis, couched in terms of disintegration and reintegration, follows an approach similar to that taken in a number of other works, notably Gabriel Almond, Scott Flanagan, and Robert Mundt, *Crisis, Choice and Change* (Boston: Little, Brown, 1973).

6. Robert Brenner, "Agrarian Class Structure and Economic Development in Pre-Industrial Europe," *Past and Present*, February 1976, pp. 52ff.

7. Wallerstein, *The Modern World System*.

8. Ibid., pp. 236-37.

9. Ibid., pp. 51, 93ff.

10. Ibid., pp. 205ff.

11. See especially Guy Fourquin, "Anciennes et nouvelles structures de sociabilité vers 1300-1500," in Pierre Léon, ed., *Histoire économique et sociale du monde* (Paris: Armand Colin, 1977), 1:260-61.

12. Edouard Perroy et al., *Le Moyen Age* (Paris: Presses Universitaires de France, 1955), pp. 369-70.

13. Wallerstein, *The Modern World System*, pp. 23-25.

14. Fourquin, "Anciennes et nouvelles structures de sociabilité," pp. 260ff.

15. The same chronology of the state is employed by Bernard Guénée, "Y a-t-il un Etat en France dès les XIV et XV siècles?" *Annales: Economies. Sociétés. Civilisations,* March–April 1971, pp. 399–406; and "Etat et nation en France au Moyen Age," *Revue Historique,* January–March 1967, pp. 17–30.

16. Wallerstein, *The Modern World System,* pp. 96ff.

17. Anderson, *Lineages of the Absolutist State,* p. 38.

18. On this topic see Jean Baechler, "Essai sur les origines du capitalisme," *Archives européennes de sociologie* 9 (1968):205–63.

19. Wallerstein, *The Modern World System,* chap. 4 and pp. 229ff.

20. Victor G. Kiernan, "State and Nation in Western Europe," *Past and Present* 31 (1965):35–36.

21. Wallerstein, *The Modern World System,* pp. 129ff.

22. Ibid., p. 208ff.

23. See Fourquin, "Anciennes et nouvelles structures de sociabilité," p. 260, and Edward W. Fox, *L'Autre France* (Paris: Flammarion, 1973), p. 62.

24. See John U. Nef, *Industry and Government in France and England: 1540-1640* (Ithaca, NY: Cornell University Press, 1967), pp. 58ff.

25. See Prosper Boissonade, *Le socialisme d'Etat* (1927), pp. 65, 216ff.

26. The state's predilections are clear from the very beginnings of absolutism: see Fourquin, "Anciennes et nouvelles structures de sociabilité." On the continuity of this policy, see Robert Mandrou, *La France aux XVIIe et XVIIIe siècles* (Paris: Presses Universitaires de France), pp. 132ff.

27. See Guy Richard, *Noblesse d'affaires au XVIIIe siècle* (Paris: Armand Colin, 1974).

28. Anderson, *Lineages of the Absolutist State.*

29. See Peter Gourevitch, "The International System and Regime Formation," *Comparative Politics,* 1978, p. 425.

30. Wallerstein, *The Modern World System,* pp. 151ff.

31. See especially Wolfram Fischer and Peter Lundgreen, "The Recruitment and Training of Administrative and Technical Personnel," in Tilly, ed., *The Formation of National States in Western Europe,* pp. 475ff; David L. Keir, *Constitutional History of Modern Britain since 1485* (London: Adam and Charles Black, 1969), pp. 7ff; Gerald E. Aylmer, *The King's Servants: The Civil Service of Charles I (1625-1642)* (New York: Columbia University Press, 1974); and Nef, *Industry and Government in France and England,* pp. 1–7.

32. Wallerstein, *The Modern World System*, p. 172.

33. Theda Skocpol, "Wallerstein's World Capitalist System: A Theoretical and Historical Critique," *American Journal of Sociology* 82, no. 5 (1977):1086. See also Nef, *Industry and Government in France and England*, p. 136, and Fox, *L'autre France*, p. 80. It is known that the annual revenue of France in the first half of the seventeenth century amounted to 80 million *livres-tournois*, whereas the annual revenue of England in the same period was only 9 million. See Nef, *Industry and Government in France and England*, p. 126.

34. Alexander Gerschenkron, *Economic Backwardness in Historical Perspective* (Cambridge: Harvard University Press, 1962), chap. 1.

35. Ibid., pp. 119-52.

36. C. Woosley Cole, *Colbert and a Century of French Mercantilism* (London: F. Cass, 1939).

37. Barry Supple, "The State and the Industrial Revolution: 1700-1914," in Carlo Cipolla, ed., *The Fontana Economic History of Europe* (Harmondsworth, England: Penguin, 1973), p. 317.

38. William Otto Henderson, *The State and the Industrial Revolution in Prussia: 1740-1870* (Liverpool: Liverpool University Press, 1958).

39. Supple, "The State and the Industrial Revolution," pp. 328ff.

40. On this subject see Jerome Blum, "The Rise of Serfdom in Eastern Europe," *American Historical Review*, July 1957, pp. 820ff; and Brenner, "Agrarian Class Structure and Economic Development," pp. 53ff.

41. See Bertrand Badie, *Stratégie de la grève. Pour une approche fonctionnaliste du PCF* (Paris: Presses de la Fondation nationale des Sciences Politiques, 1976), pp. 18-20.

42. See Claude Willard, *Les Guesdistes* (Paris: Editions Sociales, 1965), p. 350.

43. Robert Brecy, *La grève générale* (EDI, 1966).

44. Wolfgang Abendroth, *Histoire du mouvement ouvrier en Europe* (Paris: Maspero, 1967), pp. 48-9.

45. Michelle Perrot and Annie Kriegel, *Le socialisme français et le pouvoir* (EDI, 1966), p. 47.

46. Henry Pelling, *A History of British Trade Unionism* (Harmondsworth, England: Penguin, 1963).

47. See Norman Robertson and John Leslie Thomas, *Trade Union and Industrial Relations* (London: Business Books, 1968). For a comparative study of the relations among the working class, the unions, the party, and the type of state, see Colin Crouch, "The Changing Role of the State in Industrial Relations in Western Europe," in Colin Crouch and Allessandro Pizzorno, eds., *The Resurgence of Class Conflict in*

Europe (London: Macmillan, 1978), and Gérard Adam and Jean-Daniel Reynaud, *Conflicts du travail et changement social* (Paris: Presses Universitaires de France, 1978), chap. 1.

Chapter 4

1. Perry Anderson, *Passages from Antiquity to Feudalism* (London: New Left Books, 1974), and *Lineages of the Absolutist State*.
2. Elias, *La dynamique de l'occident*, p. 87. Concerning the political and social structures of feudal society, see also François Louis Ganshof, *Qu'est-ce que la féodalité?* (Brussels: Editions de la Baconnière, 1947) [English translation: *Feudalism* (Harper Torchbooks)]; and Marc Bloch, *La Société féodale* (Paris: Albin Michel) [English translation: *Feudal Society* (Chicago: University of Chicago Press, 1961)].
3. Elias, *La dynamique de l'occident*, p. 102.
4. Ibid.
5. Gerhard Ritter, "Origins of the Modern State," in Heinz Lubasz, *The Development of the Modern State* (New York: Macmillan, 1964), p. 19.
6. Anderson, *Lineages of the Absolutist State*.
7. See Brenner, "Agrarian Class Structure and Economic Development," and Skocpol, "Wallerstein's World Capitalist System," p. 1083.
8. See Gustave Dupont-Ferrier, *Les officiers royaux des bailliages et sénéchaussées et les institutions monarchiques locales en France, à la fin du Moyen Age* (E. Bouillon, 1902), pp. 274-78, where mention is made of the Cabochière Ordinance, which authorized the *bailli* to take measures to halt rural migration. On the assumption of this responsibility by the *intendants*, see Henri Regnault, *Histoire du droit français* (Sirey, 1947), p. 265.
9. Ibid., pp. 20ff. See also Lewis Mumford, *The City in History* (New York: Harcourt, Brace and World, 1961) and Charles Petit-Dutaillis, *Les communes françaises, caractères et évolutions des origines au XVIIIᵉ siècle* (Paris: Albin Michel, 1947).
10. Charles Petit-Dutaillis, *La monarchie féodale en France et en Angleterre*, p. 152.
11. Anderson, *Lineages of the Absolutist State*.
12. Ibid.
13. Dupont-Ferrier, *Les officiers royaux*, pp. 280ff and 854ff.
14. This position is not only Anderson's but also that of a whole school of English radical historians, most notably Christopher Hill and Maurice Dobb. It had been challenged by some American Marxists, particularly Paul Sweezy. On this debate, see Rodney Hilton, ed., *The Transition from Feudalism to Capitalism* (London: New Left Books, 1976).

15. Concerning relations between the bourgeoisie and the aristocracy in the Ancien Régime, see Charles Lucas, "Nobles, Bourgeois and the Origins of the French Revolution," *Past and Present*, August 1973, pp. 84–125. On the social and economic domination exercised by the rural aristocracy in France and the concomitant reinforcement of the state, see Fox, *L'autre France*, pp. 102–8 and Conclusion. See also Barrington Moore, *The Social Origins of Dictatorship and Democracy* (Boston: Beacon Press, 1966), p. 45.

16. This part of our argument shares certain points in common with the penetrating analysis of Jean-William Lapierre, who has attempted to explain the development of the state in terms of the need for social innovation. See his *Vivre sans Etat?* (Paris: Seuil, 1977), pp. 182ff.

17. On this point see Stein Rokkan, "Cities, States and Nations: A Dimensional Model for the Study of Contrasts in Development," in Eisenstadt and Rokkan, *Building States and Nations*, 1:73–96.

18. Concerning the timing of the development of a political center in England, see Petit-Dutaillis, *La monarchie féodale en France et en Angleterre*, pp. 47ff, 65ff.

19. John Gyford, *Local Politics in Britain* (London: Croom Helm, 1976), pp. 9–24.

20. Although Strayer rather curiously presents England as a case of rapid development of the state, he is forced (p. 35) to concede that, even though the political system there was centralized, it employed few civil servants, had a limited bureaucracy, and possessed institutions that were not highly differentiated from civil society (pp. 47–48). It would therefore seem more logical to speak of a political system with a low level of state development. (References are to his *Medieval Origins of the Modern State*.)

21. Ibid., pp. 18, 26, 27, 29.

22. On this point, see Denis Richet, *La France moderne: l'esprit des institutions* (Paris: Flammarion, 1973) and Louis Althusser, *Montesquieu, la politique et l'histoire* (Paris: Presses Universitaires de France, 1959).

Chapter 5

1. On this subject see Ernst Hartwig Kantorowicz, *The King's Two Bodies* (Princeton: Princeton University Press, 1957), chap. 3; and Reinhard Bendix, *Kings or People* (Berkeley: University of California Press, 1978), pp. 27–35.

2. Strayer, *On the Medieval Origins of the Modern State*, p. 16.

3. Ibid., p. 22. See also Gerd Tellenbach, *Church, State and Christian Society* (New York: Harper and Row, 1970).

4. See John S. Curtiss, *Church and State in Russia* (New York:

Columbia University Press, 1940); and Bendix, *Kings or People*, pp. 95ff.

5. See Walter Ullmann, *A History of Political Thought: The Middle Ages* (Baltimore: Penguin, 1965), pp. 35ff; and Bendix, *Kings or People*, chap. 2. The duality of the temporal and the spiritual was expressed in a variety of ways, especially in the symbol of the "two swords" Christ is supposed to have given to his disciples; the so-called "temporal sword" was used as early as the time of King Philip Augustus to justify the specific attributes of monarchical power. On this point see Regnault, *Histoire du droit français*, p. 152.

6. On the political functions of Lutheranism, see Hajo Holborn, *A History of Modern Germany, The Reformation* (New York: Knopf, 1959). On Protestantism and state building, see Stein Rokkan, "Dimensions of State Formation and Nation-Building: A Possible Paradigm for Research on Variations within Europe," in Tilly, ed., *The Formation of National States in Western Europe*, pp. 562-600.

7. See Maurice Powicke, *The Reformation in England* (New York, 1961).

8. See David Little, *Religion, Order and Law* (New York: Harper and Row, 1969), pp. 147ff.

9. Ibid., pp. 86-88, 97-98, 104.

10. Cf. Richard H. Tawney's distinction between Genevan Calvinism and English Puritanism in *Religion and the Rise of Capitalism* (New York: Mentor, 1948). On Puritan parliamentarism see J. D. Eusden, *Puritans, Lawyers and Politics* (New Haven: Yale University Press, 1958). On Puritan immigration see Peter H. Odegard, *Religion and Politics* (Oceana Publications, 1960). For an overview of all these topics see T. Sanders, *Protestant Concepts of Church and State* (New York, 1964).

11. On this point see Tilly, ed., *The Formation of National States in Western Europe*, pp. 20-21, 29.

12. On the rediscovery of Roman law, see Myron P. Gilmore, *Argument from Roman Law in Political Thought: 1200-1600* (Cambridge, England: Cambridge University Press, 1941); Kantorowicz, *The King's Two Bodies*; Guénée, *L'occident aux XIVe et XVe siècles*, pp. 94-95, 276ff; and Joseph Strayer, *Les gens de justice du Languedoc sous Philippe le Bel* (Toulouse, 1970).

13. Anderson, *Lineages of the Absolutist State*.

14. Louis Dumont, *Homo aequalis* (Paris: Gallimard, 1977), pp. 19, 44, 169; Karl Polanyi, *The Great Transformation* (Boston: Beacon Press, 1944).

15. Dumont, *Homo aequalis*, p. 25; see also Colin Morris, *The Discovery of the Individual: 1050-1200* (New York: Harper and Row, 1973).

16. Karl Polanyi, "The Economy as an Instituted Process," in Karl Polanyi, Conrad Arensberg, and Harry W. Pearson, *Trade and Markets in the Early Empires* (Glencoe, Ill.: The Free Press, 1957), pp. 243ff.

Chapter 6

1. This is one of the main themes developed by Reinhard Bendix in *Kings or People*, chap. 8.

2. See Geoffrey Barraclough, *The Origins of Modern Germany* (New York: G. P. Putnam & Son, 1963), chap. 1; Francis-Ludwig Carsten, *The Origins of Prussia* (Oxford: Oxford University Press, 1954).

3. Anderson, *Passages from Antiquity to Feudalism*.

4. See Francis-Ludwig Carsten, *Princes and Parliaments in Germany* (Oxford: Oxford University Press, 1963), p. 438.

5. Ibid., pp. 41ff.

6. See our account of Wallerstein's analysis above.

7. Roger Portal, *Les Slaves* (Paris: Armand Colin, 1965), pp. 65ff.

8. See Vassili O. Klutchevsky, *Pierre le Grand et son œuvre* (Paris: Payot, 1953).

9. Cf. Niyazi Berkes, *The Development of Secularism in Turkey* (Montreal: McGill University Press, 1964), pp. 23ff, 97ff.

10. See Ann K. S. Lambton, "Persia: the Breakdown of Society," in P. M. Holt et al., eds., *The Cambridge History of Islam* (Cambridge, England: Cambridge University Press, 1970), vol. 1A, pp. 452–54.

11. See Louis Thomas, "Dualisme et domination en Afrique Noire," in Anouar Abdel-Malek, ed., *Sociologie de l'impérialisme* (Anthropos, 1971), pp. 141–80.

12. Cf. Jean Leca and Jean-Claude Vatin, *L'Algérie politique, institutions et régime* (Paris: Presses de la Fondation Nationale de Science Politique, 1975), pp. 483ff.

13. On this subject see the analysis of John P. Nettl and Roland Robertson, *International Systems and the Modernization of Societies* (London: Faber and Faber, 1968).

14. See Fred Riggs, "Bureaucrats and Political Development: A Paradoxical View," in Joseph La Palombara, *Bureaucracy and Political Development* (Princeton: Princeton University Press, 1963), pp. 120–67.

15. See Victor Le Vine, "Le recrutement de l'élite politique et la structure politique en Afrique d'expression française," published in French translation in Birnbaum, *Le pouvoir politique*, pp. 196ff; see also Jean-François Bayart, *L'Etat au Cameroun* (Paris: Presses de la Fondation Nationale de Science Politique, 1975), pp. 216ff, 230.

16. See Huntington, *Political Order in Changing Societies*, pp. 59ff, and James C. Scott, *Comparative Political Corruption* (Englewood Cliffs, NJ: Prentice-Hall, 1972).

17. Gunther Roth, "Personal Rulership, Patrimonialism and Empire-Building in the New States," in Bendix, ed., *State and Society*, pp. 581-91. See also Jean-François Medard, "Le rapport de clientèle," *Revue française de science politique*, February 1976, pp. 103-30.

18. D. Crecelius, "Secularism in Modern Egypt," in Donald E. Smith, *Religion and Political Modernization* (New Haven: Yale University Press, 1974).

19. See Ergun Ozbudun, "Established Revolution versus Unified Revolution: Contrasting Patterns of Democratization in Mexico and Turkey," in Samuel Huntington and Clement Moore, eds., *Authoritarian Politics in Modern Society* (New York: Basic Books, 1970), pp. 380-405.

20. Immanuel Wallerstein, "Elites in French-Speaking West Africa: the Social Basis of Ideas," *The Journal of Modern African Studies* 3, no. 1 (1965):16.

21. This line of argument has been developed by the so-called "dependency theorists," most notably André Gunder Frank, *The Development of Underdevelopment*. Immanuel Wallerstein has used the same set of ideas to describe the European economic system in the early modern period: see his *Modern World System*.

22. On this subject see the work of the "transnational relations" school, particularly Robert Keohane and Joseph Nye, eds., *Power and Interdependence* (Boston: Little, Brown, 1977).

23. See Jack Goody, *Technology, Tradition and the State in Africa* (London: Oxford University Press, 1971).

24. For the definition of "organic relations" and their political consequences, see Smith, *Religion and Political Modernization*, pp. 3ff.

25. See Niyazi Berkes, *The Development of Secularism in Turkey*, p. 7; A. Sanhoury, *Le califat* (Geuthner, 1926); and Maxime Rodinson, *Marxisme et le monde musulman* (Paris: Seuil, 1972). On religion's role in maintaining the power of the sultan, see also C. Bereketullah, *Le khalifat* (Geuthner, 1924).

26. On reform movements deriving from traditional religions, see Robert Bellah, "Epilogue: Religion and Progress in Modern Asia," in Robert Bellah, ed., *Religion and Progress in Modern Asia*, pp. 207-12. On Afqāni and Abduh, see E. Kedourie, *Afqāni and Abduh* (London, 1966).

27. Concerning the Islamic notion of consensus *(ijma')* and the role it may play in adaptation to change, see Ignaz Goldziher, *Le dogme et la loi de l'Islam* (Geuthner, 1920), pp. 46ff.

Introduction to Part 3

1. Parts of this typology may also be found in J. Peter Nettl, "The State as a Conceptual Variable," *World Politics*, July 1968.

2. As part of a research effort funded by the French Centre National de Recherches Scientifiques, the Centre de sociologie politique is currently doing empirical investigations into the origins of bureaucracies, bureaucratic structures, and the people who staff them. This research has been triggered by the problems raised in the theoretical exposition in part 3 of this book, and we hope it will lead to confirmation of hypotheses touched on at various places in this work.

Chapter 7

1. See Robert Boutruche, *Seigneurie et féodalité* (Paris: Aubier, 1970) and Georges Duby, *La société aux XIe et XIIe siècles dans la région mâconnaise* (Paris: SEVPEN, 1953).

2. See Finer's interesting application of Hirschman's model to the history of absolutism in France. According to Finer, peripheral powers did in fact have three options: they could either secede (exit, according to Hirschman's terminology), rebel (voice), or rally to the monarchy (loyalty). Finer, "State Building, State Boundaries and Border Control."

3. Michael Howard, *War in European History* (Oxford: Oxford University Press, 1976), chaps. 2-4.

4. Dupont-Ferrier, *Les officiers royaux*, p. 871; concerning the careers of these officers, see pp. 229ff, 770ff.

5. Otto Hintze, "Der Commissarius und seine geschichtliche Bedeutung für die allgemeine Verwaltungsgeschicht," in Otto Hintze, *Staat und Verfassung* (Göttingen: Vandehoeck und Ruprecht, 1962), p. 275.

6. See François Olivier-Martin, *Précis d'histoire du droit français* (Paris: Dalloz, 1945); G. Chevrier, "Remarques sur l'introduction et les nécessités du 'jus privatum' et du 'jus publicum' dans les œuvres des anciens juristes français," *Archives de philosophie du droit*, 1952; and more recently, Anderson, *Lineages of the Absolutist State*.

7. Vivian R. Gruder, *The Royal Provincial Intendants* (Ithaca: Cornell University Press, 1968).

8. Andre Corvisier, *L'armée française de la fin du XVIIe siècle au ministère de Choiseul. Le soldat*, 2 vols. (1964).

9. Finer, "State and Nation-Building in Europe: The Role of the Military," in Tilly, ed., *The Formation of National States in Western Europe*, pp. 84-163.

10. On mercenaries, see Victor Kiernan, "Foreign Mercenaries and Absolute Monarchy," *Past and Present*, April 1957, pp. 66-86. Concerning the recruitment of persons with bourgeois backgrounds, see Emile G. Léonard, "La question sociale dans l'armée française," *Annales* 3 (1948):139-40.

11. See John U. Nef, *Les fondements culturels de la civilisation moderne* (Paris: Payot, 1964), p. 79.

12. Yves Durand, *Les fermiers généraux au XVIIIe siècle* (Paris:

Presses Universitaires de France, 1971); J. F. Bosher, *French Finances, 1770-1795* (Cambridge, England: Cambridge University Press, 1970); Daniel Dessert, "Finances et société au XVIIIᵉ siècle," *Annales*, July-August 1974.

13. Prosper Boissonade, *Le triomphe de l'étatisme, la fondation de la suprématie industrielle de la France, la dictature du travail (1661-1683)* (Paris, 1932).

14. Cole, *Colbert and a Century of French Mercantilism*, 2:362. On the administration of the absolutist state, see Pierre Legendre, *Histoire de l'administration de 1750 à nos jours* (Paris: Presses Universitaires de France, 1968).

15. See, for example, Alphonse Dupront et al., *Livre et société dans la France du XVIIIᵉ siècle* (1965), or Henri-Jean Martin, *Livre, pouvoirs et société à Paris au XVIIᵉ siècle* (Geneva: Droz, 1969).

16. Mandrou, *La France aux XVIIᵉ et XVIIIᵉ siècles*, p. 217.

17. Michel Antoine, *Le Conseil du Roi sous Louis XV* (Geneva: Droz, 1970).

18. Tocqueville, *L'Ancien Régime et la Révolution*, p. 122.

19. Ibid., p. 85.

20. By the close of this period, as Jacques Godechot has shown, "a series of institutions modeled on the organization of the military had erected in France an all-powerful administration with an infinite number of hierarchical echelons and which was bureaucratic in the extreme." Godechot, *Les institutions de la France sous la Révolution et l'Empire* (Paris: Presses Universitaires de France, 1951), p. 664. Concerning the reinforcement of the bureaucracy under the Directory, see C. Church, "The Social Basis of the French Central Bureaucracy under the Directory," *Past and Present*, April 1957.

21. Georges Vedel, *Droit administratif* (Paris: Presses Universitaires de France, 1961), p. 44. See also Pierre Legendre, "La royauté du droit administratif. Recherches sur les fondements traditionnels de l'Etat centraliste en France," in a special issue of the *Revue historique de droit français et étranger* (1975) devoted to "La bureaucratie et le droit."

22. Legendre, *Histoire de l'administration*, p. 385.

23. Paul Leroy-Beaulieu, *L'Etat moderne et ses fonctions* (Paris: Guillaumin, second ed., 1911), p. 520.

24. Charles Brook Dupont-White, *La centralisation* (Paris: Guillaumin, 1860), p. 188. See also Antoine Dareste de la Chavanne, *Histoire de l'administration en France et des progrès du pouvoir royal depuis le règne de Philippe Auguste jusqu'à la mort de Louis XVI* (Paris: Guillaumin, 1848). On the question of centralization in the nineteenth century, see Gabriel Lepointe, *Histoire des institutions du droit public français* (Domat-Monchrestien, 1953).

25. The literature on this subject is enormous. For a synthetic interpretation, see Pierre Birnbaum, *Les sommets de l'Etat*.

26. Tocqueville, *L'Ancien Régime et la Révolution*, p. 132.

27. François Furet, *Penser la Revolution française* (Paris: Gallimard,
1979), p. 188.

28. Richet, *La France moderne: l'esprit des institutions*, p. 161.

29. Ibid., p. 180. Contradicting himself somewhat, Richet also
asserts that what we call "public office" was so inextricably bound up
with the person who occupied that office that it is impossible to trace
the history of a particular post or council without writing the history
of the individuals who occupied the post or presided over the council
(ibid., p. 79), which amounts to denying the existence of a well-defined
system of roles.

30. Bernard Le Clerc and Vincent Wright, *Les préfets du Second
Empire* (Paris: Armand Colin, 1972), p. 57. See also Theodore Zeldin,
The Political System of Napoleon III (New York: Macmillan, 1971).

31. Pierre Grémion, *Le pouvoir périphérique* (Paris: Seuil, 1976);
Jean-Claude Thoenig, "La relation entre le centre et la périphérie en
France," *Bulletin de l'IIAP*, November–December 1975.

32. Pierre Birnbaum et al., *La classe dirigeante française* (Paris:
Presses Universitaires de France, 1978).

33. See Hans Rosenberg, *Bureaucracy, Aristocracy and Autocracy.
The Prussian Experience: 1660–1815* (Cambridge: Harvard University
Press, 1958), pp. 43, 44, 199.

34. In this respect the *Landrat* seems rather like local notables in
England who filled public offices. As John Gillis has noted, the pro-
fessionalization of the bureaucracy took place within a very authoritar-
ian context and in a closed social milieu, largely noble. *The Prussian
Bureaucracy in Crisis: 1840–1860* (Stanford: Stanford University
Press, 1971), p. 212.

35. Rudolf Braun, "Taxation, Sociopolitical Structure and State-
Building: Great Britain and Brandenburg-Prussia," in Tilly, ed., *The
Formation of National States in Western Europe*, pp. 243–327.

36. Wolfram Fisher and Peter Lundgreen, "The Recruitment and
Training of Administrative and Technical Personnel," in ibid., pp.
456–561. See especially pp. 545ff.

37. Moore, *The Social Origins*, p. 442; Gustav Schmoller, *The
Mercantile System and its Historical Significance Illustrated Chiefly
from Prussian History* (New York: Macmillan, 1902); William Otto
Henderson, *The State and the Industrial Revolution in Prussia, 1740–
1870*; Wolfram Fischer, "Government Activity and Industrialization
in Germany (1815-1870)," in Walt W. Rostow, ed., *The Economics
of Take-off into Sustained Growth* (London: Macmillan, 1963); Supple,
"The State and the Industrial Revolution, 1700-1914."

38. Otto Mayer, *Le droit administratif allemand* (Giard et Briere, 1903), p. 82.

39. Weil, *Hegel et l'Etat*, pp. 103-4.

40. Armstrong, *The European Administrative Elite*, pp. 165ff. Senior civil servants in France are better versed in economics.

41. Thomas Ellwein, *Das Regierungssystem der Bundesrepublik Deutschland* (Westdeutscher Verlag Opladen, 1977); Wolfgang Zapf, "Führungsgruppen in West- und Ostdeutschland," in Wolfgang Zapf, ed., *Wandlung der deutschen Elite. Ein Zirkulationsmodell deutsche Führungsgruppen, 1919-1961* (Munich, 1965); see also Klaus von Beyme, *Die politische Elite in der BRD* (Munich: R. Piper, 1971).

42. Zapf, "Führungsgruppen," p. 19.

43. Bärbel Steinkemper, *Klassische und politische Bürokraten in der Ministerialverwaltung der BRD* (Cologne: C. Heymanns, 1974).

44. Paolo Farnet, *Sistema politico e società civile* (Turin: Giappichelli, 1971); Sidney Tarrow, *Partisanship and Political Exchange* (London: Sage, 1974); L. Graziano, "La crise italienne," *Revue française de science politique*, April 1977.

Chapter 8

1. George M. Trevelyan, *The History of England*.

2. Finer, "State Building, State Boundaries and Border Control," p. 119.

3. Kantorowicz, *The King's Two Bodies*.

4. Aylmer, *The King's Servants*.

5. David Bayley, "The Police and Political Development in Europe," in Tilly, ed., *The Formation of National States in Western Europe*, pp. 328-79.

6. Henry William Wade, *Administrative Law* (Oxford: Clarendon Press, 1971).

7. See Mario Losano, *I grandi sistemi giuridici* (Turin: Il Mulino, 1978).

8. Tom Nairn, "The Decline of the British State," *New Left Review*, April 1977, p. 12. As far as Keith Thomas is concerned, there is no real state in Great Britain today: see his "United Kingdom," in Raymond Grew, ed., *Crises of Political Development in Europe and the United States* (Princeton: Princeton University Press, 1978), p. 82.

9. Barry Supple, "The State and the Industrial Revolution, 1700-1924," in Carlo Cipolla, ed., *The Fontana Economic History of Europe*, 3:313.

10. Ian Weinberg, *The English Public Schools: The Sociology of Elite Education* (New York: Atherton, 1967).

11. William MacKenzie and J. Grave, *Central Administration in Britain* (London: Longman, 1957); David Roberts, *The Victorian Origins of the British Welfare State* (New Haven: Yale University Press, 1960); Moses Abramovitz and Vera Eliesberg, *The Growth of Public Employment in Great Britain* (Princeton: Princeton University Press, 1957).

12. Ernest Barker, *The Development of Public Services in Western Europe, 1660-1930* (London: Oxford University Press, 1944), and Fisher and Lundgreen, "The Recruitment and Training of Administrative and Technical Personnel," are among the few comparative studies of bureaucracy available.

13. Edgar Gladden, *Civil Services of the United Kingdom, 1855-1970* (London: Cass, 1967); Peter Self, *Administrative Theories and Politics* (London: Allen and Unwin, 1973).

14. Danielle Loschak, *La fonction publique en Grande-Bretagne* (Paris: Presses Universitaires de France, 1972), p. 5.

15. Armstrong, *The European Administrative Elite*.

16. Pierre Birnbaum, "Institutionalization of Power and Integration of Ruling Elites: A Comparative Analysis," *European Journal of Political Research*, 1978, pp. 108-9.

17. John Urry and John Wakeford, *Power in Britain* (London: Heinemann, 1973).

18. W. L. Guttsman, "Elite Recruitment and Political Leadership in Britain and Germany since 1950: a Comparative Study of MPs and Cabinets," in Philip Stanworth and Anthony Giddens, eds., *Elites and Power in British Society* (Cambridge, England: Cambridge University Press, 1974); R. W. Johnson, "L'élite politique britannique, 1955-1972," in Birnbaum, *Le pouvoir politique*.

19. Ivor Crewe, *Elites in Western Democracy* (London: Croom Helm, 1974).

20. Louis Hartz, *The Liberal Tradition in America* (New York: Harcourt, Brace & Co., 1955); Charles and Mary Beard, *Basic History of the United States* (New York: Doubleday, 1944).

21. Albert Pollard, *Factors in American History* (Cambridge, England: Cambridge University Press, 1925), pp. 31-33.

22. Samuel Huntington, "Political Modernization: America vs. Europe," in Bendix, *State and Society*, pp. 193, 196.

23. Seymour M. Lipset, *The First New Nation* (New York: Doubleday, 1967).

24. See Richard Hofstadter, *The American Political Tradition and the Men Who Made It* (New York: Knopf, 1948) and *Social Darwinism in American Thought* (Boston: Beacon, 1955); M. Fishwick, *American Heroes: Myth and Reality* (Washington, 1954); Gerhard Lenski, *The*

Religious Factor (New York: Doubleday, 1961); Pierre Birnbaum, *La structure du pouvoir aux Etats-Unis* (Paris: Presses Universitaires de France, 1971).

25. Charles Beard, *An Economic Interpretation of the Constitution of the United States* (New York: Free Press, 1965).

26. R. Zweigenhaft, "Who Represents America?" *Insurgent Sociologist* 5, no. 3 (1975).

27. G. William Domhoff, *The Powers That Be: Processes of Ruling Class Domination in America* (New York: Random House, 1979), pp. 160–61.

28. Thomas Dye, *Who's Running in America?* (Englewood Cliffs, NJ: Prentice-Hall, 1976), p. 157; Beth Mintz, "The President's Cabinet, 1897–1973: A Contribution to the Power Structure Debate," *Insurgent Sociologist* 5, no. 3 (1975):135.

29. Domhoff, *The Powers That Be*, chaps. 2 and 3.

30. Frederik Ogg and Perley Ray, *Le gouvernment des Etats-Unis d'Amérique* (Paris: Presses Universitaires de France, 1958), chaps. 3 and 4.

31. On the history of the civil service in the United States, see Gérard Conac, *La fonction publique aux Etats-Unis* (Paris: Armand Colin, 1958).

32. Bernard Schwartz, *Le droit administratif américain* (Sirey, 1952); Ferdinand Stone, *Institutions fondamentales du droit des Etats-Unis* (LGDJ, 1965), part 4, chap. 1; Edward Farnsworth, *An Introduction to the Legal System of the United States* (New York: Oceana, 1963), especially p. 150.

33. François and Claire Masnata, *Pouvoir, société et politique aux Etats-Unis* (Paris: Payot, 1970), part 2, chap. 2.

34. See for example Jean Rivière, *Le monde des affaires aux Etats-Unis* (Paris: Armand Colin, 1973), pp. 80ff. Even an author like Charles Lindblom, a eulogist of pluralism and polyarchy, asserts that "businessmen thus become a kind of public official and exercise what, in a broad view of their role, are public functions." *Politics and Markets* (New York: Basic Books, 1977), p. 172.

35. David Stanley, Dean Martin, and Jameson Doig, *Men Who Govern* (Washington, DC: Brookings Institution, 1967), pp. 34ff.

36. L. Nigro and K. Meier, "Executive Mobility in the Federal Service: A Career Perspective," *Public Administration Review*, May–June 1975, p. 294.

37. Pierre Birnbaum, "La place des hauts fonctionnaires dans l'élite du pouvoir aux Etats-Unis. A propos de la théorie de Mills," *Revue française de science politique*, August 1973.

38. Theodore Lowi, *American Government: Incomplete Conquest* (Hinsdale, IL: Dryden Press, 1976).

39. Arend Lijphart, "Consociational Democracy," *World Politics,* January 1969, p. 219. See also Gerhard Lembruch, "A Non-Competitive Pattern of Conflict Management in Liberal Democracies; the Case of Switzerland, Austria and Lebanon," in Kenneth McRae, ed., *Consociational Democracy: Political Accommodation in Segmented Societies* (Toronto: McClelland, 1974).

40. Arend Lijphart, *The Politics of Accommodation: Pluralism and Democracy in the Netherlands* (Berkeley: University of California Press, 1968), pp. 198–99.

41. See Brian Barry, "Political Accommodation and Consociational Democracy," *British Journal of Political Science,* October 1975.

42. Uli Windisch, *Lutte de clans, lutte des classes* (Lausanne: L'Age d'homme, 1976). The authors shows that, even today, conflicts are resolved by clan struggle rather than class struggle.

43. See Dusan Sidjanski, "Environnement politique en Suisse," in Dusan Sidjanski et al., *Les Suisses et la politique* (Berne: Peter Lang, 1975); Jurg Steiner, *Amicable Agreement versus Majority Rule: Conflict Resolution in Switzerland* (Chapel Hill, NC: University of North Carolina Press, 1974).

44. Marcel Bridel, *Précis de droit constitutionnel de la Suisse* (Payot, 1965).

45. Jean-François Aubert, *Petite histoire constitutionnelle de la Suisse* (Neuchatel, 1974). See also François and Claire Masnata-Rubatel, *Le pouvoir suisse, séduction démocratique et répression suave* (Christian Bourgeois, 1978).

46. William Martin, *Histoire de la Suisse* (Lausanne, 1966), p. 265.

47. Paolo Urio, "Aspects de la fonction publique en Suisse," *Annuaire international de la fonction publique, 1971–1972,* p. 414.

48. U. Kloti, *Die Chefbeamten der schweizerischen Bundesverwaltung: Soziologische Querschnitte in den Jahren 1938, 1955, und 1969* (Berne: Francke, 1972), p. 177. In this respect Switzerland is just as close to Germany and Italy as to the United States.

49. See Erich Gruner et al., *L'Assemblée fédérale suisse, 1920–1968* (Berne, 1970); and, especially, Henry Kerr, *Parlement et société en Suisse* (Geneva: Department of Political Science, mimeographed, 1977).

50. Theda Skocpol has also shown how the state finds the source of its own transformation within itself. See *States and Social Revolutions: A Comparative Analysis of France, Russia, and China* (Cambridge, England: Cambridge University Press, 1979), pp. 284–86.

Index